• *Studies in American Biblical Hermeneutics 6* •

The Second Naiveté

Barth, Ricoeur, and the New Yale Theology

• *Studies in American Biblical Hermeneutics 6* •

The Second Naiveté

Barth, Ricoeur, and the New Yale Theology

□ ◻ ◻ ◻ □

by
Mark I. Wallace

MERCER

ISBN 0-86554-380-1   MUP/P089

The Second Naiveté. Barth, Ricoeur, and the New Yale Theology.
Second edition
Copyright ©1990, 1995
Mercer University Press, Macon, Georgia 31210-3960 USA
All rights reserved
Printed in the United States of America

□ □ □

□ □ □

Library of Congress Cataloging-in-Publication Data
Wallace, Mark I., 1956–   .
The second naiveté :
Barth, Ricoeur, and the new Yale theology / by Mark I. Wallace.
xvi+130pp. 6x9" (15x23 cm.).
(Studies in American biblical hermeneutics ; 6).
Includes bibliographical references and index.
ISBN 0-86554-380-1 (pbk.; alk. paper).
1. Bible—Hermeneutics.
2. Bible—Criticism, interpretation, etc.—History—20th century.
3. Barth, Karl, 1886–1968—Contributions in biblical hermeneutics.
4. Ricoeur, Paul—Contributions in biblical hermeneutics.
5. Bible—Theology—History—20th century.
6. Bible—Theology. 7. Revelation.
I. Title. II. Title: New Yale theology. III. Series.
BS476.W32   1995   90-322249
220.6'01—dc20   CIP

•CONTENTS•

• EDITOR'S PREFACE •

At its core, the enterprise of American biblical hermeneutics is dialog-ical or dialectical in character. It attempts to bring into conscious focus the interplay between the biblical texts and the American reader. It does not try to *establish* anything; rather, it attempts to *uncover* what is already present in the interpretive process in our time and place. Meaning, in other words, is not understood as a one-way street, leading from text to reader. It is a back and forth, a give-and-take, a *negotiation*. At various times in the process, the culturally bound text dominates. At other times, it is the reader—similarly bound in her or his own culture—that exhibits the up-per hand. In either instance meaning is a product of the transaction be-tween text and reader, building in large part on what the two parties bring to the experience of a shared communication.

This book by Mark Wallace captures the essence of the dialogical ap-proach to human knowledge. It does so in terms of content, but perhaps more important, it also does so in terms of spirit. It is an intrinsically American theological work as a result. Wallace considers three distinctive hermeneutical traditions: that inspired by the theology of Karl Barth, the interpretive theory of Paul Ricoeur, and the common presumptions of what he terms the "new Yale theologians." He believes that embedded in the intratextual dynamic afforded by these three twentieth-century tra-ditions lies a powerful hermeneutical blueprint that could revitalize American theological reflection in our time and place. Wallace achieves this through an extended constructive and sympathetic dialogue with Barth, Ricoeur, and the Yale theologians. Yet, this is not the blind follow-ing of the true believer. Wallace, in fact, reads his three sources exactly in the manner that the very hermeneutical theory that he advocates de-mands, in the hope and expectation that they might add significantly to the synthetic wholeness that our critical or postcritical world has relin-quished. It is an approach that embodies the very title of this volume, the approach of a *second naiveté*. And, as the final chapter makes evident, he does so successfully and in a provocative way.

Deconstruction, or postmodern critical theory, is not an enemy that Wallace engages with this book. In fact, the book does not project the concept of enemies as such, unless it be that common enemy, the creeping irrelevance of theological reflection in our society. Rather, Wallace maintains that those theologians who have taken up the cause of deconstruction and the death of God, while correctly grasping the significance and necessity of overcoming biblical naiveté, have too quickly relinquished the distinctive resource of biblical faith for our society. Notwithstanding such critical realities as the intentional fallacy and the relatively impoverished knowledge produced by the historical sciences, Wallace steadfastly builds the case that the Bible remains the center of Christian thought and the source by which we might renew *it* and *ourselves* in the process. The problem is how to recover the historic centrality of the Bible for the Christian faith while fully participating in the contemporary world in both its intellectual and everyday senses. To answer this issue, he turns to Barth, Ricoeur, and the Yale theologians and their common rejection of the absoluteness of the historical-critical methodologies that have dominated mainstream biblical interpretation in our era. Wallace builds upon the insight shared by these theological sources—that it is not enough to establish the meaning of the Bible in *its* historical place and time. Our time is as important a theological resource in gaining meaning from the Bible as its own time. While we cannot control the meaning of the Bible— Barth said that we are objects of the biblical message and not its subjects—we must not understand it merely as a history book, since it is fundamentally a book *for us*.

In the last analysis the real issue with which this book wrestles is whether or not we can return to the Bible in hope and expectation for a meaningful understanding of life *after* our critical sensibilities have been awakened by the Enlightenment. Certainly this is a question for Western civilization as a whole; and it is especially an issue for the American culture at whose birth the Enlightenment served as midwife. Theologically, at the heart of this matter lies the staking out of new ground for the category of revelation. Revelation must imply in some sense that the Bible is Other than us, that its voice is not our voice. The force of the critical methodologies spawned by the philosophy of the Enlightenment, especially those which have mushroomed in our time, has been to seek out the similarities of the biblical texts with other texts. The Bible, it has countlessly been shown, is one religious Scripture among other Scriptures. Doubtlessly such similarities exist. But does such knowledge end the matter? Is this sort of criticism the last word? Wallace finds such an approach unsatisfying, and as a result, he opens new vistas of understanding by which we can both affirm the critical heritage of the Enlightenment and go beyond it as well.

Finally, it can hardly escape the knowledgeable reader that of the two primary theologians that frame the central issues of this book—Barth and Ricoeur—only Ricoeur has labored significantly within the American cultural context. Perhaps as a result, two essential features of Ricoeur's thought give him more of an "American feel" than Barth: (1) the polyphony of biblical revelation (as opposed to Barth's christocentric hermeneutics), and (2) a thoroughgoing theological cosmology (as opposed to Barth's anthropocentric interpretive stance). Yet, it is not Wallace's intention to argue for any sort of general superiority of Ricoeur over Barth based on "Americanism." Rather, he (as well as Ricoeur himself) is careful to point out the widespread impact Barth's thought has made upon all theological reflection in our century. By his work in this volume, Wallace captures the best spirit of American biblical hermeneutics and provides a solid model for it.

Charles Mabee
Marshall University

• REVISED PREFACE •

Beyond the desert of criticism, we wish to be called again.
—Paul Ricoeur, *The Symbolism of Evil*, 351

Christianity has always been a religion of the book. Differences in creed and temperament, substance and style, generally have been mediated by appeals to the common documentary source of the churches, the Bible. Though many Christian communities are splintered by numerous theological, historical, ethnic, and other differences, the Bible continues to function as a unifying force just insofar as it provides the basic grammar, so to speak, that shapes the Christian vision of the world. But if the Bible can be said to perform this unifying role, it must also be said that the Jewish and Christian scriptures have functioned as well to fissure and divide people from one another by engendering disparate, even incommensurate understandings of reality. For a contemporary theology that seeks biblical fidelity, the question then arises whether the theologian can interpret the Bible as providing a body of coherent truths to live by, or whether the Bible's complexity and plurality finally dooms to failure any attempt to read the Bible from the perspective of a master narrative or central ideal. The struggle to answer this question is the animating spirit of this book. Central to this project, therefore, is the problem of interpretation, the problem of understanding how meaning can be made out of the heterogeneity of the biblical texts.

Interpretation always involves risks. We may encounter a text with a certain set of presuppositions as to its meaning only to find those presuppositions unwarranted in light of a further understanding of the text's subject matter. This can be an uncomfortable and unnerving process, and yet when the slippage does occur between initial presuppositions and subsequent readings the possibility arises for new and more adequate interpretations to present themselves to open-minded communities of inquiry. This book had its origin in the space opened by a comparative reading of a group of thinkers whose positions have been conventionally located at different points along the theological spectrum. It began with the wager that some of the more seminal theological thinkers of our time have not been adequately understood because their contributions have been studied in opposition, rather than in relation, to one another. The result has been a lack of cross-fertilization between scholars of different intellectual orientations and a certain sterility in contemporary theological discourse and education. The time has come for a fresh reappraisal of positions that many have considered only in relative isolation from one another.

As much as any other single factor, Karl Barth's thought and legacy has created the factional spirit that characterizes some of the theological work done today. His acerbic genius so dominated the middle third of this century that theologians were pressed into choosing sides and maintaining allegiances: one either traveled with Barth or against him. Those who journeyed with Barth were aided by the compass of his attack on liberalism and the well-marked roadmap of his developing *Church Dogmatics*, which, along with his other writings, carefully plotted out what could and could not be said about God and God's self-disclosures in salvation-history. Those who did not take this path pursued a variety of other perspectives (neoliberalism, neo-Thomism, process theology, death-of-God theology, and so forth) that did not command the attention and readership that was directed toward Barth's revival of the Protestant Reformation heritage.

In retrospect, it now seems that the differences between Barthians and non-Barthians were so sharp because both groups tacitly accepted Barth's self-interpretation of his own project, namely, a dismantling of the neo-Protestant foundations that had supported Christian life and thought since the Enlightenment. In fact, however, Barth was only partly successful in his efforts. He had to stand on something as he pulled out the neo-Protestant supports, and, as many have now recognized, what he stood on was the very theological substructure to which his most pointed criticisms had been directed. When the angle of vision shifts away from Barth's purported intentions and toward his actual achievement, what we see is a theological itinerary that bears some remarkable resemblances to the liberal Protestant theologies of the nineteenth-century that Barth so vigorously resisted. The important differences notwithstanding, a number of contact points exist between Barth and his liberal predecessors: a conflicted appropriation of historical criticism in theological studies; the Kantian notion that theology should be a descriptive rather than a metaphysical enterprise; the thesis that revelation is a self-authenticating, *sui generis* phenomenon; and the adoption of the modernist principle that all theology, as Barth said in agreement with Schleiermacher, should be an ellipse with two foci, "Christ and Man." Minimally this indicates a common sensibility on some critical issues between Barth and his theological precursors—a sensibility, to risk oversimplification, more concerned with what the Bible means today than with what it once said, more concerned with the Christ of Scripture than the God of the religions, and more concerned with humankind's relationship with God through revelation than with epiphanies of the sacred through nature. What is at stake, then, in this revisionary interpretation of Barth's continuation of aspects of the liberal heritage is not only judicious Barth scholarship, as important as that is, but also a way of doing theology that can mediate some of the divisions (divisions inspired, in part, by Barth's combative style) that permeate much of today's creative theological reflection. Part of the burden of this volume is to offer a mediating voice in this ongoing dispute. Now that the ties of intellectual continuity between Barth and his precursors are being made we can move on to the task of building communication between Barth and other thinkers that before we might have regarded as opponents of one another, not potential dialogue partners.

One such dialogue partner for a revised conversation with Barth is Paul Ricoeur. Both Barth, the biblical theologian who sought to reawaken the Reformation tradition, and Ricoeur, the philosopher with a deep-seated Reformed Christian identity, seek to uncover the Word in the words of the biblical witness; as Ricoeur says, to grasp "God as the one who addresses himself to me and who therefore can be grasped in the Event of the Word alone" (letter to author, 24 September 1984). Initially, then, I will argue here that Barth and Ricoeur, in spite of their many differences, share a common *commitment* to the subject matter of the biblical texts as the primary source for theological reflection, and a related hermeneutical *method* for interpreting this subject matter. As a point of entry into both thinkers, I have chosen the discipline of hermeneutics and Ricoeur's idea of the second naiveté. I define the former as the study of what readers do when they seek to understand the meaning of literary texts (in this case, the biblical texts), while the notion of the second naiveté here stands for a critically mediated attitude of expectation towards the reality-claims of religious faith (in this case, the faith exercised within the biblical environment).

The book's basic thesis, therefore, is that the hermeneutical programs of both Barth and Ricoeur seek to release a thoughtful openness toward the "world" portrayed in the biblical witness. The world of the text for both thinkers is neither what traditional biblical critics investigate as the historical or authorial background *behind the text*, nor, as some post-modernist readers of the Bible argue, is it the self-contained and indeterminate play of meaning *within the text* that suspends all claims to referring to the "real" outside of the text. The world of the text, rather, is the literary and theological subject matter *in front of the text* that potentially can liberate a "critical" (Barth) or "second" (Ricoeur) naiveté toward the text's claims on the reader's life and thought. Against the grain of historical criticism's disinterest in the text's theological subject matter and poststructuralism's antireferential poetic is Barth's and Ricoeur's concern for allowing the Bible to redescribe reality through its own compelling modes of discourse.

This thesis is developed in the book's first three chapters. Chapter 1 describes Barth's exegetical method as a successful interweaving of theology, historical criticism, and literary theory. As a "metacritical" hermeneutic that seeks robust fidelity to the biblical subject matter, Barth's thought bears important affinities with the deconstructionist interest in the free play of discourse while repudiating the historicist focus on the authorial and cultural milieus that produced the biblical texts. As test cases for the practical success of Barth's hermeneutic, I have examined in this context his typological exposition of the Levitical scapegoat and the "kinship" between Judas and Paul.

Analogous to Barth's operative assumption that the Bible is a trustworthy mediation of the divine Word, chapter 2 argues that Ricoeur's thought begins with the Kantian hope, the existential wager, that the Bible has successfully "named God" and that this naming compels the philosopher of language to read and interpret the discourse where this has occurred. What the reader/believer finds is that this discourse is not a rhetorical frame that simply houses the Bible's core message, but the driving dynamic force that makes that message work and that produces its rich meaning. Instead of regarding the biblical discourses as obsolete figurations of the world (Bultmann) or as occult detours into a semantic abyss (Kermode), Ricoeur reads the Bible as an ensemble of competing improvisations on the "real" precisely because, and not in spite of, its diverse literary genres. What, if any, exegetical fruit this thesis bears is examined with reference to Ricoeur's recent exposition of the Gospel of Mark.

Chapter 3 is a comparative study of Barth and Ricoeur that begins with an analysis of the tripartite hermeneutical method employed by each thinker. Biblical interpretation follows an arc that commences with a first construal of the text as a whole (understanding); a further explication of the text's constituent parts in relation to the whole (explanation); and a final mediation between the parts and the whole that allows for a transfer of the text's world into the world of the reader (appropriation). The goal is to follow the text's referential intention toward its distinctive ontology, its vision of the real, through the play of narrative strategies and tropological twists within the text. After passing through, but never around, the first innocence of original understanding and the desert trial of rigorously examining the text's parts, the reader is asked to risk reading the text critically and naively once more—to become adult critic and naive child, as Ricoeur says—in order to resituate one's life and understanding within the horizon of the text's "reality." Yet while Barth and Ricoeur formally share this threefold strategy for interpreting the biblical world, we will see in this chapter that they materially interpret the content of this world so differently that the dialogue between them carried out to this point will now appear limned with major difficulties, perhaps intractable difficulties. The balance of chapter 3, therefore, considers the conflict between Barth's anthropocentric and Christocentric construal of the biblical subject matter in relation to Ricoeur's cosmological and theocentric reading of the same.

Chapter 4 introduces another voice, the so-called new Yale theology, into the conversation between Barth and Ricoeur. I have taken the liberty of labeling this theology a school or movement because of the family resemblances that exist among the postliberal theological proposals of Hans Frei, Paul Holmer, and George Lindbeck. Notwithstanding their differences, the Yale theologians agree on the exigency for a theology that is constructed out of the narrated world of the New Testament and that resists the temptation to translate this world into extrascriptural categories for the sake of Christianity's conversation with its cultured despisers. At first glance this position may seem to situate the Yale approach closer to Barth than to Ricoeur (who is criticized by Frei et al. for being a liberal foundationalist). I will suggest instead that Ricoeur's notion of *dépouillement* (self-divestment) frees his hermeneutic from this criticism and relocates it on the same antifoundational footing that is shared by Barth and the Yale theologians. Nodding to Barth, the chapter concludes with a discussion of the Yale School's ambiguity concerning the precise status of Christian truth-claims: do such claims provide us with reliable access to the world outside of the Bible, however tenuous this access may be, or are they circumscribed within an intratextual horizon that has no purchase on reality *extra nos*?

In the light of this three-way conversation, the final chapter suggests that a revival of the idea of revelation is the challenge for theology today. If the wager of the book is to be successful, if a hermeneutic of the second naiveté is a viable option for our time, then the dialogue opened up in the previous four chapters must be pressed into the service of articulating how the biblical witness can remake and refigure reality through its conflicted play of multiple discourses. If the Bible is regarded only as a problem to be demythologized, a historical artifact to be dissected, or a self-enclosed aesthetic object to be played with, it will lose its power to speak again and renew the foundations of Western culture. Is it possible that the biblical texts could be used again to refigure and reinvigorate the world around us? And if such a venture is possible, could we not find that the struggle to build meaningful communities of hope and resistance would be aided greatly by a critical and engaged reading of these texts? Such is the hope of this volume.

I acknowledge the following journals and thank their editors for permission to revise and reuse the papers as cited: "Parsimony of Presence in Mark: Narratology, the Reader, and Genre Analysis in Paul Ricoeur," *Studies in Religion/Sciences Religieuses* 18 (1989); "Karl Barth's Hermeneutic: A Way Beyond the Impasse," *The Journal of Religion* 68 (1988); "Theology Without Revelation?" *Theology Today* 45 (1988); "The New Yale Theology," *Christian Scholar's Review* 17 (1987); and "The World of the Text: Theological Hermeneutics and Biblical Interpretation in the Thought of Karl Barth and Paul Ricoeur," *Union Seminary Quarterly Review* 41 (1986).

Finally, I am indebted to the many friends and colleagues who originally made this book possible:
—to my dissertation committee at the University of Chicago (Brian Gerrish, Langdon Gilkey, and David Tracy);
—to Paul Ricoeur for conversations and correspondence concerning the viability of the interpretations of his thought offered here;
—to the many critical readers of the manuscript in its parts or as a whole: Robert Almeder, Garrett Green, George Hunsinger, Walter Lowe, Angel Medina, Gerald McKenny, George Stroup, Alex Vishiom, and the editorial staff at Mercer University Press;
—to the many students at Georgia State University and Swarthmore College who have provided me with a rich community of theological reflection;
—to Charles Mabee for his unflagging support without which, I fear, this book would never have seen the light of day; and
—to Ellen Ross, my partner in thought and whimsy, for her encouragement of this project from first plantings to fruition.

Mark I. Wallace
Swarthmore College

June 1995

THEOLOGICAL HERMENEUTICS AND KARL BARTH

*[To accept Scripture as] God's revelation . . . does not mean an annul-
ling of the results of biblical scholarship in the last centuries, nor does it
mean a breaking off and neglect of efforts in this direction. What it does
mean is a radical re-orientation concerning the goal to be pursued, on the
basis of the recognition that the biblical texts must be investigated for their
own sake to the extent that the revelation which they attest does not stand
or occur, and is not to be sought, behind or above them but in them.*[1]

• The Centrality of the Word •

The ongoing interest in the relationship between hermeneutics and
Christian theology can be attested to by the number of books and articles
published on the subject during our time.[2] These studies have promoted

---

[1]Karl Barth, *Church Dogmatics*, vol. 1:2, trans. G. T. Thomson and Harold Knight
(Edinburgh: T. & T. Clark, 1956) 494.

[2]See *inter alia* Hans Frei, *The Eclipse of Biblical Narrative: A Study in Eighteenth
and Nineteenth Century Hermeneutics* (New Haven: Yale University Press, 1974), and
The Identity of Jesus Christ: The Hermeneutical Bases of Dogmatic Theology (Philadelphia: Fortress Press, 1975); Sallie McFague, *Metaphorical Theology: Models of God in
Religious Language* (Philadelphia: Fortress Press, 1982); Edgar V. McKnight, *Meaning in Texts: The Historical Shaping of a Narrative Hermeneutics* (Philadelphia: Fortress Press, 1978); Ted Peters, "Hermeneutical Truth and Theological Method,"
Encounter 39 (1978): 103-23; Lynn Poland, *Literary Criticism and Biblical Hermeneutics* (Missoula MO: Scholars Press, 1985); Anthony C. Thiselton, *The Two Horizons:
New Testament Hermeneutics and Philosophical Description* (Grand Rapids MI: Wm.
B. Eerdmans Publishing Co., 1980); David Tracy, *The Analogical Imagination: Christian Theology and the Culture of Pluralism* (New York: Crossroad Press, 1981); Charles
M. Wood, *The Formation of Christian Understanding: An Essay in Theological Hermeneutics* (Philadelphia: Westminster Press, 1981); as well as the numerous books
and articles on the subject by Paul Ricoeur, many of which are referred to in this
book.

the dialogue between interpretation theory in philosophy, literary criticism, and the social sciences, on the one hand, and hermeneutical inquiries in theology and biblical studies, on the other. It is unfortunate, however, that Karl Barth's hermeneutical thought is sometimes given short shrift in this discussion because his theology is regarded as being either unconcerned with, or even hostile to, hermeneutical issues.[3] Edgar V. McKnight, for example, in deference to post-Bultmannian hermeneutics and current literary criticism, passes over Barth's thought as having little, if anything, to contribute to contemporary hermeneutics.[4] Peter Stuhlmacher comments similarly that Barth's opposition to a singular historical-critical analysis of the biblical texts prevents him from seeing the depth of the hermeneutical problem.[5] More pointedly, Anthony C. Thiselton trades on the common misunderstanding of Barth as pneumatic exegete and argues that his emphasis on the Spirit in interpretation so separates human understanding from divine revelation that the task of hermeneutics is scuttled altogether.[6]

Though I find these readings of Barth ill informed, there is a grain of truth in these evaluations insofar as Barth probably would have scoffed at labeling his thought "hermeneutical." As we know from Eberhard Busch's biography of Barth, the Swiss theologian cast derision on hermeneutics as another short-lived academic vogue.[7] Barth would probably have directed the student interested in the rapprochement between hermeneutics and theology to his Marburg colleague, Rudolf Bultmann, and deferred the task of hermeneutical theology to one who could "sail nearer to the wind of time"[8] than he.

[3]Hans Frei's and Charles Wood's work, as well as George Stroup's *The Promise of Narrative Theology* (Atlanta: John Knox Press, 1981), are significant exceptions to this general rule. Other excellent studies of Barth in particular include David Paul Henry's *The Early Development of the Hermeneutic of Karl Barth as Evidenced by His Appropriation of Romans 5:12-21* (Macon GA: Mercer University Press, 1985); and David Ford's "Barth's Interpretation of the Bible," in *Karl Barth: Studies of His Theological Methods*, ed. S. W. Sykes (Oxford: Clarendon Press, 1979) 55-87, as well as his published Cambridge dissertation (*Barth and God's Story: Biblical Narrative and the Theological Method of Karl Barth in the "Church Dogmatics"* [Frankfurt am Main and Bern: Peter Lang, 1981]).

[4]McKnight, *Meaning in Texts*, 65-72.

[5]Peter Stuhlmacher, *Historical Criticism and Theological Interpretation of Scripture*, trans. Roy A. Harrisville (Philadelphia: Fortress Press, 1977) 51.

[6]Thiselton, *Two Horizons*, 87-92.

[7]See Barth's disparaging comments to this effect in Eberhard Busch, *Karl Barth: His Life from Letters and Autobiographical Texts* (Philadelphia: Fortress Press, 1975) 466-94.

[8]While his attitude was certainly in keeping with the intellectual climate of the

If this is the case, why are the current summary treatments of Barth's hermeneutic misguided? If Barth seems to have little, if any, interest in hermeneutical issues, what constructive insights on the topic could he have to offer? In this chapter I will suggest that Barth's writings on theological hermeneutics deserve our attention because of their firm grasp of the interpretive guidelines operative in discerning the meaning of the biblical witness to the Word of God. Barth is a consummate hermeneut in his handling of traditional Christian and scriptural themes, his fulminations about the mistaken enterprise of hermeneutics notwithstanding. From his early discovery of a way of interpreting the "new world of the Bible" in 1916, to the exegetical guidelines announced in the *Römerbrief* and systematically developed in the *Church Dogmatics*, Barth's hermeneutical method as well as his actual exegetical performance warrant further study.

To understand Barth's theological hermeneutic, one must first grasp his doctrine of the Word of God. This category not only provides the foundation for his hermeneutic but also the main support for his theological project as a whole. Such a claim, however, confronts an immediate difficulty. Can we really organize Barth's theology around his understanding of one idea, namely, the Word of God? It is always difficult with a theologian of Barth's intellectual range to specify the "center" or "essence" of such a theologian's work. In the breadth of its scope and the systematic organization of its topics, his thought does not lend itself well to attempts to uncover any one unified rule that can be said to govern its individual parts.

Yet numerous attempts have been made to uncover something like a unifying theme in Barth's theology, ranging from the Word of God, the Trinity, the Holy Spirit, grace, justification, and Jesus Christ, to his political theology, doctrine of time, exegetical method, and notion of the Wholly Other.[9] These diverse attempts to specify the organizing princi-

---

postwar era, Barth felt that Bultmann's attempt to read the New Testament with an existentialist hermeneutics was a "cold" and "humorless" enterprise that purchases contemporary relevance of the Christian message at the price of fidelity to the subject matter of the biblical world. See Busch, *Karl Barth*, 386-91.

[9]Stephen Sykes, "Barth and the Power of the Word," chap. 8 in *The Identity of Christianity* (Philadelphia: Fortress Press, 1982); Eberhard Jüngel, *The Doctrine of the Trinity: God's Being in Becoming*, trans. H. Harris (Grand Rapids MI: Wm. B. Eerdmans Publishing Co., 1976); Phillip J. Rosato, *The Spirit as Lord: The Pneumatology of Karl Barth* (Edinburgh: T. & T. Clark, 1985); G. C. Berkouwer, *The Triumph of Grace in the Theology of Karl Barth* (London: S.P.C.K., 1956); Hans Küng, *Justification: The Doctrine of Karl Barth and a Catholic Reflection*, rev. ed. (Philadelphia: Westminster Press, 1964); Hans Urs von Balthasar, *The Theology of Karl Barth*, trans. John Drury (New York: Holt, Reinhart and Winston Publishing Co., 1971);

ple of Barth's theology cast needed, if only partial, rays of light on the vast topography of his thought. Barth, however, mistrusted the temptation of commentators to uncover a systematic principle in his theology. To elevate such a principle in isolation from Barth's other dogmatic loci threatens to undermine the goal of all his theological work: the free expression of God's Word apart from any controlling definition of the essence of Christianity.[10] As secondary forms of God's Word, the Bible and church proclamation mediate to the interpreting community the founding Word of God in Jesus' life and message; it is this Word in its tripartite form—as Christ, preaching, and Scripture—that is self-evidentially the "basis, foundation, and center" of Christian theology.

> [The] object, which must dictate theological method, is the Word of God itself. It is not a conception of it. It is not, therefore, a basic dogma, tenet, principle, or definition of the essence of Christianity. It is not any kind of truth that can be controlled. Dogmatics certainly has a basis, foundation, and centre. But—and we must remember this point, especially when we are thinking of the autonomy of dogmatics—this centre is not something which is under our control, but something which exercises control over us. The autonomy in which dogmatics has to choose its method must consist solely in the recognition of its theonomy, i.e., in its free submission to the sovereignty of the Word of God alone.[11]

Barth's theology seeks to be theonomously governed by its free submission to the Word of God—the "center" of Christian theology that "is not something under our control, but something which exercises control over us."[12] The focal point of his theology is a nonsystematic "center" that has the capacity to decenter and reorient our expectations as to how it should normatively function in Christian dogmatics. Barth envisions theology as alternately grounded in its fidelity to its true center, the Word of God, but nevertheless fragmented and partial in its attempts to maintain this center. Barth's category of the Word of God is the most reasonable point of entry into this theology and into his theological hermeneutic as well.

Friedrich Wilhelm Marquardt, "Socialism in the Theology of Karl Barth," in *Karl Barth and Radical Politics*, ed. and trans. George Hunsinger (Philadelphia: Westminster Press, 1976); R. H. Roberts, "Karl Barth's Doctrine of Time: Its Nature and Implications," in *Karl Barth: Studies of His Theological Methods*, 88-146; Ford, "Barth's Interpretation of the Bible," 55-56; Stephen G. Smith, *The Argument to the Other: Reason beyond Reason in the Thought of Karl Barth and Emmanuel Levinas* (Chico CA: Scholars Press, 1983).

[10]Barth, *Church Dogmatics* 1:2, 853-84.

[11]Ibid., 886.

[12]Ibid.

Barth never seeks to demonstrate the reliability of the Bible as a form for the Word of God because he axiomatically presumes Scripture to be a faithful witness to the divine event. "We will not ask: why the Bible? and look for external grounds and reasons. We will leave it to the Bible it-self . . . to vindicate itself by what takes place [in it]."[13] Recent insights in philosophical hermeneutics are analogous to Barth's position here. As Hans-Georg Gadamer notes, literary works that are true classics have a certain "acquired authority," even though there is no empirical test or measure by which the reliability of this authority can be conclusively demonstrated; rather, the classic presents itself as true to a community of interpretation already persuaded by its view of things. Indeed, this authority "rests on the recognition," as Gadamer says, that these works contain a "better understanding" of reality than that which we have apart from these classics.[14] For Barth, Scripture has a similar status; the truth of the Bible is a recognizable, authoritative, time-tested perspective on reality superior to our own. The Bible proves and "vindicates itself,"[15] as Barth says; it convincingly presents the truth in such a decisive way that the human response is simply one of gracious obedience. This, then, is the fiduciary component of Barth's hermeneutic: Scripture is trusted because in the past and the present it has functioned as a faithful witness to the divine reality by virtue of its role as God's Word written.

Only those who accept this axiom and have been "gripped" by the biblical subject matter can adequately interpret Scripture. If the Bible claims to be revelatory, then it should be read as such and interpreted accordingly. Barth acknowledges the circularity of this claim, but maintains that without the operative presupposition that the Bible mediates the Word of God no sound hermeneutic can be sustained. Many biblical scholars and theologians, however, have criticized Barth's inner-Christian starting point as being uncritical, even fideistic. They have sought a more publicly warranted and objective exegetical method that does not demand, a priori, a positive answer to the very question at issue, the Bible's claim to be the Word of God.[16] Barth's retort is that without our initial confidence in this claim, theological hermeneutics is undermined because the scriptural words are not read on their own terms as a true witness to the divine Word. He continues by saying that any notion of an

---

[13]Barth, *Church Dogmatics* 1:2, 506.

[14]See Hans-Georg Gadamer, *Truth and Method,* trans. Garret Barden and John Cumming (New York: Continuum Press, 1975), esp. sections entitled "The Rehabilitation of Authority and Tradition" and "The Classical Example," 245-58.

[15]Barth, *Church Dogmatics* 1:2, 506.

[16]See Van A. Harvey, *The Historian and the Believer* (Philadelphia: Westminster Press, 1966) 19-37, 153-63.

objective and presuppositionless hermeneutic that brackets the biblical claim to revelation not only fails at the outset to respect its subject matter, but also is a quixotic and humorous impossibility that cannot be realized by historical subjects who do not begin their exegesis in a vacuum. "There is a notion that complete impartiality is the most fitting and indeed the normal disposition for true exegesis, because it guarantees a complete absence of prejudice. For a short time, around 1910, this idea threatened to achieve almost canonical status in Protestant theology. But now we can quite calmly describe it as merely comical."[17]

The ideal of an unbiased hermeneutic is a red herring that legitimizes our failure to allow Scripture to impose on us an *epoche* or check against our all-too-human refusal to risk an interpretation of the biblical words as an occasion for the revelatory Word. Under the guise of a presuppositionless hermeneutic, we gainsay the necessary presupposition of any adequate biblical hermeneutic—that God speaks through these texts—and fail to submit our understanding to the understanding of the text.

> It is only as those who are mastered by the subject matter, who are subdued by it, that we can investigate the humanity of the word by which it is told to us. The sovereign freedom of this subject matter to speak of itself imposes on us in the face of the word as such and its historicity an *epoche*, of which there can be no inkling if we presuppose the comical doctrine that the true exegete has no presuppositions, and against which we consistently and most flagrantly offend if we presuppose that doctrine.[18]

Barth's hermeneutical sophistication is apparent in his dismissal of non-presumptive exegesis as a "comical" avoidance of our situation-bound interpretations of classic texts such as the Bible. Along with many philosophical hermeneuts of today, he recognizes the perspectival and prejudicial character of all interpretive work (including biblical exegesis) that seeks fidelity to the subject matter in question.

• The Use of Historical Criticism •

Theological hermeneutics is characterized today by the debate between historical criticism and literary criticism in biblical studies. Is the Bible best understood diachronically as a historical document with identifiable traditions and origins? Or is it best studied synchronically as a literary text with structural and semantic features? Some critics do exegesis solely from one perspective or the other.[19] Yet others argue that only in

---

[17]Barth, *Church Dogmatics* 1:2, 469.

[18]Ibid., 470.

[19]For an overview of the current discussion, see Bernard C. Lategan, "Some Unresolved Methodological Issues in New Testament Hermeneutics," in *Text and Reality*, Bernard C. Lategan and Willem S. Vorster (Atlanta: Scholars Press, 1985) 3-26.

the integration of both the historical and literary approaches in an explicitly theological hermeneutic can the proper aim of biblical interpretation be realized: the understanding of the biblical words as a new Word of address for the modern reader.

Barth's hermeneutic is a powerful, if controversial, resource in resolving the debate surrounding this conflict of approaches. Of course, many contemporary exegetes and theologians have noted the importance of correlating critical methods and the theological interpretation of Scripture.[20] Yet Barth's theological hermeneutic seems to be especially well equipped for this task because it consistently marshals the insights of both historical studies and close textual analysis in order to further a theological construal of the whole sweep of the biblical drama. Barth's struggle to discern anew the Bible's theological intent is not a dismissal of modern scholarship,[21] but an attempt to critique, combine, and deepen the historical and literary approaches through a unifying theological framework—a framework that acknowledges the power of the biblical texts to mediate the Word of God to the reader. Using an exegetical model that reflects the trinitarian character of his theology— interpretation is empowered by the Spirit's witness to God's self-disclosure in Christ, the Word in the words of the biblical writings—he challenges the present-day working assumptions of both historical criticism (the Bible is primarily intelligible in relation to the historical situation within which it was written) and literary criticism (the Bible should be read as prose fiction and devoid of any stable extralinguistic referent). Barth's hermeneutic points us beyond the cul-de-sac that results from regarding historical criticism and literary analysis in isolation from a thoroughgoing theological use of Scripture.

To begin, what was Barth's understanding of historical criticism, and how does his theological hermeneutic improve on the singular use of the historical method in biblical studies?

Such a question begs the issue according to Barth's earliest detractors, however, who maintained that his hermeneutic was not an advance beyond the discipline of scientific exegesis but a retreat to the precritical biblicism of an earlier era. They contended that his *Romans* commentary was an irresponsible and cavalier attack on the scientific gains the historical-

---

[20]Brevard Childs's canonical criticism, for example, dialectically relates historical criticism and theological interpretation. See *The New Testament as Canon* (Philadelphia: Fortress Press, 1984) esp. 3-53. Unlike Barth, however, Childs does not exercise the same literary freedom to read the Bible as a complicated typological intertext, a topic I will explore below.

[21]Then and now, however, this argument persists. For the earlier debate, see n. 22. Among others in the present context, see Harvey, *Historian and the Believer*, 153-63, and Thiselton, *Two Horizons*, 88-90.

critical study of the Bible had made in German academic circles since the pioneering work of J. S. Semler (1725–1791) and J. P. Gabler (1753–1826). His critics argued that his theological reading of the New Testament dismissed all too easily the then-emerging consensus concerning the role historical reconstructions of the Bible's *Sitz im Leben* should play in explaining the original meanings of the biblical documents. Barth was merely a biblicist and pneumatic exegete, they argued, who naively interpreted the New Testament as a Spirit-inspired book. The criticism, in effect, was that Barth abandoned the critical task of evaluating the Bible in the light of its Near Eastern parallels and antecedents in order to glean from it timeless ideas that could conveniently support his own theological and dogmatic presuppositions.[22]

The debate was intense, and Barth fought his opponents' charges. He consistently maintained that he was not an opponent of the historical method in biblical studies: "I am not an enemy of historical criticism."[23] His complaint was never against historical criticism per se but against its historicist bias—the appeal to the historical world behind the Bible instead of the subject matter within the Bible. Barth avers that real criticism does not stop at the threshold of historical inquiries into the language, background, and authors of the Bible; rather, it presses forward to understand better the text as a message concerning God's relationship to humankind. He recognizes that the Bible is not an ahistorical, authorless text, but, by the same token, the thrust of the scriptural message is missed if the Bible is read exclusively in the light of its ancient world origins and not in relation to its own inner-Christian starting point. The Bible's works contain *Deus dixit* written. Like any other classic text, the Bible should be read on its own terms as speaking about something that is worthy of our attention. "I have, moreover, no desire to conceal the fact that my 'Biblicist' method—which means in the end no more than 'consider well'—is applicable also to the study of Lao-Tse and of Goethe."[24] "Consider well" is the true epithet for Barth's hermeneutic: interpretation is guided by the text's power to bring its unique subject matter face-to-face with the reader.

Barth's commentators labeled his early theology "dialectical" because of its tensions between God and humanity, salvation and history, time and eternity, theology and philosophy, and so on. His early hermeneutic operates with the same polarizing logic: "The matter contained in the text cannot be released save by a creative straining of the sinews, by a relent-

---

[22]For the early interchange between Barth and his critics, see James M. Robinson, ed., *The Beginnings of Dialectic Theology* (Philadelphia: Westminster Press, 1968).

[23]Karl Barth, *The Epistle to the Romans*, trans. Edwyn C. Hoskins from the 6th German ed. (Oxford: Oxford University Press, 1933) 90.

[24]Ibid., 12.

less, elastic application of the 'dialectical' method."[25] In the prefaces to the *Romans* commentary, he maintains a dialectic between *Wort* and *Worten*, *Sache* and *Urkunde* to underscore that the Bible as a product of human discourse is nevertheless a medium of a special subject matter or Word that demands our attention and energy if it is to be understood. The goal, then, is not simply to *explain (Erklärung)* the text vis-à-vis its historical background but to *understand (Verstehen)* the text as bearing an important message as well. "The Word *(Wort)* ought to be exposed in the words *(Worten)*. Intelligent comment means that I am driven on till I stand with nothing before me but the enigma of the matter *(Sache)*; till the document *(Urkunde)* seems hardly to exist as a document."[26]

Barth's mature hermeneutic in the *Church Dogmatics* continues the dialectic introduced in the *Romans* commentary between the biblical words and the realities signified and made real by these words. Study of the text's authors and the text's history is an important "prolegomenon" to understanding the world of the text, but it is not itself that understanding.[27] As important as "knowledge of the biblical men" and the Bible's "historical circumstances" is for disclosing the critical historylike events that inaugurated the biblical witness, such knowledge still must be rejected as "an interpretation of the Bible— and on the very ground that it does not take the human work of the Bible as seriously as according to the Bible itself it ought to be taken."[28] A truly historical and critical reading of the Bible will take seriously Scripture's self-understanding as a testimony to revelatory events. Barth always had a taste for irony: it was the historical critics, not he, who were insufficiently critical because they would not risk an interpretation of the biblical words' central claim to be a faithful attestation to the divine Word. As in the *Romans* commentary, Barth argues that a thoroughly radical historical-critical approach will not stop with the Bible as merely a collection of history-specific words, but will seek to uncover the meaning of these words as witnesses to revelation.

True criticism lies in the exposition of the matter *(Sache)* in the document *(Urkunde)*. This hermeneutical principle, Barth argues, is not the special province of theological hermeneutics because any attentive reading of a text will attest to the same rule. Thus, Barth's provocative observation: "There is no such thing as a special biblical hermeneutics."[29] The

---

[25]Ibid., 8.

[26]Ibid. See also Georg Eichholz, "Der Ansatz Karl Barths in der Hermeneutik," in *Antwort: Karl Barth zum Siebzigsten Geburtstag,* ed. Rudolf Frey, et al. (Zollikon-Zürich: Evangelischer Verlag AG, 1956) 52-58, for a clear analysis of this hermeneutical dialectic in Barth's *Romans* commentary.

[27]Barth, *Romans,* 6-9.

[28]Barth, *Church Dogmatics* 1:2, 467.

[29]Ibid., 466.

rule that Scripture says something "does not alter the fact that this principle is necessarily the principle of all hermeneutics, and that therefore the principle of the Church's doctrine of Holy Scripture, that the Bible is the witness of divine revelation, is simply the special form of that universally valid hermeneutical principle."[30] All interpretation, biblical or otherwise, should be guided by the subject matter of the text. "The universal rule of interpretation is that a text can be read and understood and expounded only with reference to and in light of its theme."[31] As straightforward as this rule may seem, its neglect by modern biblical scholars, according to Barth, was one of the major causes of the church's anemia in the twentieth century. This is the problem of historicism in the historical-critical method—the emphasis on the Bible's historical situation at the expense of its theological message:

> The idea against which we have to safeguard ourselves at this point is one which has tacitly developed in connection with modern theological historicism. It is to the effect that in the reading and understanding and expounding of the Bible the main concern can and must be to penetrate past the biblical texts to the facts which lie behind the texts. Revelation is found in these facts as such (which in their factuality are independent of the texts).[32]

The problem of historicism notwithstanding, Barth maintained that historical criticism was an indispensable tool in the hermeneutical task. His goal was to adapt critically and deepen the historical method, not dispense with it. Consider his discussion in *Church Dogmatics* 3 concerning the Genesis creation accounts as prehistorical, narrative *Sage*.[33] These early sagas are retrospective historylike accounts of a special type: etiological narratives that imaginatively reconstructed Israel's founding events on the basis of their authors' later encounters with Yahweh. Barth's taxonomy of the creation stories was not original; in this he borrowed freely from the form critical studies of Genesis by Gunkel and Eichrodt, among others.[34]

What distinguishes Barth's approach from that of his biblical colleagues was his controlling desire to understand better the theological intent of these stories—that the created order is where God uniquely

---

[30]Ibid., 468.

[31]Ibid., 493.

[32]Ibid., 492.

[33]Ibid., 3:1, 42-329.

[34]See Walther Eichrodt, *Theology of the Old Testament*, trans. J. A. Baker from the 6th German ed., 2 vols. (Philadelphia: Westminster Press, 1961, 1967), and Hermann Gunkel, *The Legends of Genesis*, trans. W. H. Carruth (New York: Schocken Books, 1964).

fashions a covenant relationship with humankind. With the form critics, Barth uses in his exegesis the provocative parallels between Genesis and the Gilgamesh epic: the cosmic struggle between good and evil, the personification of the Deity, the feminine imagery for the earth. Yet while sharing important formal similarities with the Babylonian myths, the Genesis accounts historicize these myths by locating them within the concrete history of Israel. So the Genesis accounts are truly saga—not positivist history or timeless myth. Barth's classification of Genesis 1-2 as saga and recognition of their similarities and differences with Babylonian legends—insights derived from the Old Testament scholars of his time—set the stage for his theological insight that God meets humankind in a particular, covenantal history that has as its basis and presupposition the one-time work of creation. His historical work is written with an eye to the particular creation-covenant theology announced in the opening chapters of Genesis. In this way, Barth held, the time-bound (but never timeless) creation stories can become the medium for revealing God's abiding and present concern for the human species.

Barth's focus on the text's theological subject matter explains his virtual lack of concern with the issue of authorial intention in the interpretation of Scripture. His hermeneutic avoids what is sometimes called the "intentional fallacy," in which the author's stated or uncovered intention in writing a text is considered to be the primary criterion for any valid interpretation.[35] As works of public discourse, texts are not private extensions of an author's interior life; they are not controlled by the determinate intentions of their authors. An author's intentions are no longer accessible in any language-neutral fashion once they are structured under the linguistic rules of composition and genre that govern all literary works. What the text means is not equivalent to what the author intended it to mean; hence the question concerning how best to uncover and discern the author's intentions in writing a particular text is beside the point. The point is to interpret the text, not the author, and let the text say something to the reader above and beyond what the author might have intended it to say.

> The understanding of [an other's word] cannot consist merely in discovering on what presuppositions, in what situation, in what linguistic sense and with what intention . . . the other has said this or that. . . . My expression cannot possibly consist in an interpretation of the speaker. Did he say something to me only to display himself? I should be guilty of shameless violence against him, if the only result of my encounter with him were that I now knew him better than before. What lack of love! Did he not say something to me at all?[36]

---

[35]See Paul Ricoeur, *Interpretation Theory: Discourse and the Surplus of Meaning* (Fort Worth: Texas Christian University Press, 1976) 25-26.

[36]Barth, *Church Dogmatics* 1:2, 464-65.

The text and the author are not the same thing— "interpretation of the speaker" or author behind the text is not convertible with interpretation of the text itself. Even if we have some linguistically mediated access to what an author might have intended to mean by writing this text, we do not thereby understand all that the text can possibly mean for the contemporary situation in its interaction with other texts, modes of composition, and distinctives of genre and style.

Rudolf Smend regards Barth's hermeneutic to be an example of postcritical exegesis. In an influential article on Barth's interpretation theory, Smend argues that Barth's scriptural exegesis should not be situated in the period of precritical interpretation nor in the current period of historical-critical methods.[37] Barth's exegesis rather belongs to "a postcritical period, in which Scripture can be read naively *again*."[38] The value of Smend's argument is its understanding of Barth's hermeneutic as rejecting a wholesale reintroduction of ancient and Reformation theological uses of Scripture in total opposition to current scholarly biblical studies. In one sense, Barth's method is postcritical: it utilizes and adapts historical criticism to enable a second, yet critical, openness on the part of the interpreter to the world of the biblical witness.

Barth protested against Smend's reading of his position, arguing that his procedure was not postcritical but really and authentically critical because it sought to use all forms of biblical criticism (those that are naive and those that are modern) in the service of understanding the Bible's true object, the Word of God in Jesus Christ.[39] Substituting his own terminology for Smend's, Eberhard Jüngel suggests that Barth's hermeneutic is "metacritical" rather than postcritical: Barth seeks to unify historical criticism and theological interpretation in order to further the work of understanding Scripture's unique subject matter.[40] As metacritical, not postcritical, Barth's hermeneutic is more thorough and critical than the historical method itself because it subjects all forms of hermeneutical inquiry (especially those that seek consistency with scientific methods) to

---

[37]Rudolf Smend, "Nachkritische Schriftauslegung," in *Parrhesia: Karl Barth zum achzigsten Geburtstag*, ed. Eberhard Busch, et al. (Zürich: EVZ Verlag, 1966) 215-37.

[38]Ibid., 218.

[39]The passage Smend cites from *Church Dogmatics* in support of his argument—Barth's exegetical excursus on nos. 13-14 in 4:2, 478-83—does not yield Smend's threefold division of the history of hermeneutics in the context of Barth's thought. While such a division may in fact obtain in the development of biblical interpretation, it is not a division that adequately describes Barth's project—a project that sought to be truly critical, not postcritical.

[40]Eberhard Jüngel, "Theologie als Metakritik: Zur Hermeneutik theologischer Exegese," in his *Barth-Studien* (Zürich and Cologne: Benziger Verlag, 1982) 91-98.

the written Word of God as the final arbiter of the text's meaning. The dynamic and living Word of the text critiques and relativizes all our best attempts at understanding this Word.

Barth is not an enemy of historical criticism. His concern, rather, is to harness the historical method as an aid in serving the goal of all biblical exegesis: the theological interpretation of Scripture. The value of historical criticism lies in its ability to disclose the founding events that gave rise to the early communities of biblical faith and discourse. This is no mean feat, and Barth welcomes the historian's facility for allowing us to reexamine diachronically the primal events and testimonies that occasioned the formation of Israel and the early church. Yet, because this historical work is not enough, Barth's ultimate goal is to coordinate both the investigative work of the historian and the hermeneutical work of the theologian in order to enable a "second, or better, a new naiveté" for the interpreter in response to the Bible's strange and unique subject matter.[41]

• The Promise of Theological-Literary Interpretation •

Up to this point, we have seen that Barth's hermeneutical concern is to link the study of the Bible's historical background with the exposition of its theological message. In short, he correlates that text's *Sitz im Leben* with its *Sitz im Wort*, with the emphasis on the latter. In this we see a fundamental affinity between Barth's antihistoricist hermeneutic and current literary interpretations of the Bible: that is, the Bible's meaning is not located in the historical realities or authorial intentions *behind* the text, but in the language-specific realities spoken of *within* the text.[42] Barth stands alongside both New Critical and current deconstructive critics of the Bible in maintaining that all literary creations, the Bible included, are primarily works of art, not by-products of history. As such, they possess a life of their own, a life relatively independent from the cultural and authorial milieus that produced them. Possessing semantic autonomy, the "literary work exists, in a sense, outside of history, in a kind of aesthetic preserve"[43] where the text's surplus of meaning escapes the finite conditions that gave rise to it in the first place.

"Outside of history" the Bible is not a static "artifact" whose determinate origins make its meaning easily accessible; it is rather a profoundly complicated "intertext" in which competing modes of discourse, literary styles, and compositional strategies openly play with, dislocate, and effect change upon one another. The Bible's interlocking words, gen-

---

[41]Ibid., 98.

[42]See Barth, *Church Dogmatics* 1:2, 494.

[43]Lynn Poland, "The New Criticism, Neoorthodoxy, and the New Testament," *Journal of Religion* 65 (1985): 472.

res, and referents weave together a new textual dynamism that may have little to do with the combination of initial historical and creative factors that obtained at the place, and during the time in which, it was originally written. Within Barth's primary focus on the Bible's message, there is a remarkable openness to the plurality of theological meaning in Scripture. Barth freely interprets the Bible as a figural, tropological, typological intertext—as a crisscrossing of veiled and sundry figures and types that anticipate and allude to one another. With remarkable sophistication, Barth highlights the imaginative literary dynamics that carry the meaning of the Bible's central characters and incidents. In this section, I will consider the relation of Barth's method to contemporary literary readings of the Bible by way of first examining one Old Testament and then one New Testament example of his typological hermeneutic.

In his lucid history of doctrine, Jaroslav Pelikan argues that classical Christian exegetes took one of two attitudes toward the Jewish Bible in order to claim it as their own Old Testament Scripture: either the Hebrew texts were stratified into theologically binding and legally nonbinding material, or they were systematically rethought allegorically and typologically as containing figures of Christ and the Gospel.[44] The obvious Marcionlike danger of the first attitude was that because no clear and consistent lines of division could be drawn between the different sections, the church risked the danger of losing the Mosaic law's moral and theological dimensions through its disregard for the law's ceremonial aspects. Hence, the chosen method for a hermeneutical retrieval of the Hebrew Scripture as the church's book was initially provided by allegorical exegesis, at least until the time of the Enlightenment. Pelikan's historical observation has implications, however, beyond the patristic period to which it was directed. The history of Christian theology's reception of the Old Testament has always been, implicitly or explicitly, an identification with either one or both of these two positions in some form or another. The church's early struggles to appropriate as its own the sacred literature of Judaism remains with us today: do we read the Old Testament selectively as containing some relevant and some irrelevant materials, or do we read it typologically as being consistently relevant to Christian theology (though only by its analogy with the New Testament)?

Modern theology since the Enlightenment has favored some variation on the stratification method when it has sought to appropriate the Old Testament theologically. Understandably, most modern theologians are puzzled, if not downright embarrassed, by the exegetical liberties taken by their precritical predecessors who typologically saw Christ and Chris-

---

[44]See Jaroslav Pelikan, *The Emergence of the Catholic Tradition (100-600)*, vol. 1 of *The Christian Tradition: History of the Development of Doctrine* (Chicago: University of Chicago Press, 1971) 11-27.

tian themes foreshadowed throughout the Old Testament. As responsible readers of the Bible who seek at all costs not to do Christianizing violence to the biblical texts, contemporary exegetes and theologians, if they look to the Old Testament at all, see it as a culture-bound historical document whose religious significance lies not—as the pre-Enlightenment theologians thought—in its clear (albeit anticipatory) Christ-centered message of salvation for the church, but in its remarkable stories about Israel and Israel's God.

"Whether we like it or not, the Christ of the New Testament is the Christ of the Old Testament, the Christ of Israel."[45] Against the grain of modern biblical and theological scholarship, Barth opted for the second perennial hermeneutical option vis-à-vis the Old Testament bequeathed to us by classical theology: typological exegesis. Barth's ready use of typological exegesis today may seem to us anachronistic at best and irresponsible at worst. As moderns, we may not want to follow Barth's Old Testament exegesis, but the Swiss theologian's logical rigor on this issue confronts us with an uncomfortable choice. If, as Christian exegetes, we take seriously the New Testament's claim to provide the definitive fulfillment of the Hebrew Bible's messianic expectations in the person of Christ ("You search the scriptures . . . and it is they that bear witness to me," John 5:39), then one of the ways by which we can productively retrieve the message of the Old Testament is to read it spiritually as a prefiguration of the New Testament gospel. We may not opt for such a thoroughgoing typological overreading of the Old Testament as does Barth, but if we grant that such a reading is sometimes legitimate (and how can we not do so if we regard the Old Testament not simply as a record of Israel's faith, but as a Word for the church today?), is not our disagreement with Barth not a disagreement over the *kind* of precritical, typological exegesis he practices, but only over the *degree* to which he uses it with as little restraint as did the church's traditional exegetes?

Church Dogmatics 1 announces Barth's intentional recovery of the typological method for Christian dogmatics as a corrective to the "religio-historical" interpretation of the Old Testament that had then dominated modern biblical exegesis and much of academic theology. Barth avers that only when the whole Bible is read as pointing to Christ—the fulfillment of the Old Testament witness—can we grasp Scripture's "true object and content." "A religio-historical understanding of the Old Testament in abstraction from the revelation of the risen Christ is simply an abandonment of the New Testament and of the sphere of the Church in favor of that of the Synagogue, and therefore in favor of an Old Testament which is understood apart from its true object and content."[46]

---

[45]Barth, *Church Dogmatics* 2:2, 488.

[46]Ibid., 489.

But it is not until *Church Dogmatics* 2 that Barth's typological approach is given wide register. Part 1 of this volume begins by speaking of the knowledge of God as a possibility founded on the readiness of God to reveal concretely God's self in Christ. The knowledge of God follows the reality of God, which Barth defines in this half-volume as the one who loves in freedom. Barth concludes 2:1 with a discussion of the perfections or attributes of God, which he groups under a series of contrapuntal pairs: grace and holiness; mercy and righteousness; patience and wisdom; unity and omnipresence; constancy and omnipotence; and eternity and glory.

Barth continues his doctrine of God in 2:2 by further specifying the act of the One who loves in freedom as the election of grace (and concludes by drawing out the ethical implications of this act). Barth's doctrine of election is one of his most novel and persuasive revisions of the theological tradition. He understands divine graciousness toward us in terms of the specific electing activity of the God witnessed to in Scripture. Election is defined with reference to Jesus Christ as the subject and object of election: Jesus Christ as the Son of God is both the electing God (subject) and, as the Son of Man, the elected human being (object). Christ's election graciously includes all people within it because Christ is the one who both elects humankind for God and elects himself to bear our suffering so as to make our election to God possible.

In God's election of Jesus Christ for all humankind, God elects a single community that in Christ mediates the divine election to us. This one community has two forms: Israel and the church. In the form of Israel, the community stands for God's deserved judgment of our sin; as the church, the community represents God's undeserved mercy toward us in Jesus Christ who, as Israel's Messiah and the church's Lord, is the living unity underlying both forms of the one community. But God in Christ does not just elect a general community for salvation. God's care for us as individuals is demonstrated by the divine election of specific persons. God chose one human person, Jesus Christ, to bear and cancel our debts, and in turn Christ relates to us as individuals in our election of grace. Barth's hermeneutic presumes the election of the One who elects himself to be the Elect of God and the Rejected of God so that all of us as individuals are included in this single reality of God's forgiving, unmerited grace.

• Typology in Leviticus and Paul •

Church Dogmatics 2:1, §35.2, "The Elect and the Rejected," contains an exegetical excursus on Leviticus 16 in support of Barth's position that Christ is the basis of unity for our initial rejection, and subsequent election, by God. This excursus is a lucid example of Barth's typological interpretation of the Old Testament. He begins by noting that the Day of Atonement ritual discussed in Leviticus 16 revolves around the symbolism of two goats: one is chosen for the Lord to be sacrificed on the mercy-seat as an offering for the people's sin, while the other is driven into the wilderness as a scapegoat that carries away the people's sin. Barth regards this story of ritual purification to be a "sign and testimony of the divine intention" for Israel.[47] The treatment of the two creatures symbolizes God's relationship to Israel: Israel is represented both by the goat accepted by God as a sacrifice and by the goat rejected by God as a transfer-object for Israel's transgressions. On another level, however, Israel's ritual is ours as well because now all humankind is pictured in the Old Testament as both elect and nonelect, both chosen by God as acceptable and rejected by God as unworthy. (In fact, all the great narrative sagas of the Old Testament structurally demonstrate this binary opposition: God favors Abel but not Cain; God chooses Isaac and expels Ishmael; God prefers Jacob over Esau, Rachel over Leah, Joseph over his brothers, David over Saul, and so on). Barth acknowledges that while the Israelites did not fully understand the symbolism of their own Day of Atonement, not every detail of this rite will make sense to us either. "Just as no Israelite could recognize himself directly in the slaying of the first creature, so none could recognize himself directly in the expulsion or release of the second. In the latter aspect, too, what the picture portrays transcends the human reality known to us in this aspect as well."[48]

So the point of this ritual story is not to offer a one-to-one allegorical correspondence between God's grace and our salvation, but to give a "picture" in broad strokes of how God relates to Israel (and us). We cannot comprehend the magnitude of God's grace apart from such stories: "This reality can only be attested by these stories, as by the ritual described in the passages. It can be addressed to man only in the form of a picture."[49] Barth's hermeneutic upholds the unity of Scripture's subject matter (content) and its modes of literary expression (form): we learn about God's ways through stories apart from which we cannot comprehend the mystery of divine activity.

Leviticus 16 tells us about Israel and it tells us about ourselves, the elected and rejected of God. But this ritual story also works on a third level by spiritually referring to the source and ground of Israel's and our election and rejection, Jesus Christ, even though the Christ-referent for this passage is not immediately apparent. Though the passage appears to intend one referent as the subject matter of the ritual—one individual, according to Barth, who symbolizes Israel's and, by implication, all humankind's rejection and acceptance by God—it is not clear who or what this one referent could be. "We are faced, therefore, by a twofold enigma in connection with the subject of the Old Testament witness. On the one

---

[47]Barth, *Church Dogmatics* 2:2, 357.

[48]Ibid., 362.

[49]Ibid.

hand, it consists of the inscrutability of the death and life of the man to whom both the sacrificial rituals . . . refer. On the other hand, it consists of the inscrutability of the unity of this man."[50] Barth recognizes that the Levitical ceremonial practice may not mean anything at all to some readers, that its determining referent is inscrutable, and therefore that its ancient rituals of blood sacrifice could be reasonably construed as having "no subject at all, that its testimony points into the void."[51] But if the whole Bible has a Word for the church today, any part of the Bible—even a part dealing with ancient Jewish ritual—cannot be abandoned as inscrutable and without determinate meaning. He maintains that the story of the two sacrificial goats makes little sense unless the rite is read as pointing beyond itself to something else. But what is this something else? Given the remarkable parallelisms between the incidents of the story and the life of Christ—like the first goat, Christ must shed his blood to be a spotless offering for the many, and like the second goat, he must become the rejected scapegoat that bears the sins of the many—the Christian exegete can responsibly "trope" the Levitical rituals as speaking ultimately of Christ.

Barth, therefore, presents us with two options in the interpretation of Leviticus 16: either we read the passage as finally signifying an "unknown quantity," a "void" with no clear "subject," or we read it as referring to Jesus Christ, "the true and proper subject of the Old Testament witness."[52] I find Barth's presentation of these two options to be a fruitful anticipation of the current hermeneutical debates between traditionalist and deconstructionist interpreters of literary texts. Following Augustine, traditionalists maintain that semantic units such as words and sentences signify extralinguistic objects with determinate meanings. In this scheme biblical literature is read as capturing the truth of things by offering faithful transcriptions of historical persons and events. While the traditionalists acknowledge that some forms of written and spoken discourse do employ rhetorical and tropological figures in order to adorn the facts accessible to language, they still maintain that straightforward descriptions and declarations about the world, such as "I have forgotten my umbrella," intend or refer to a specifiable object and occasion a delimited number of interpretations.

Deconstructionist critics, on the other hand, argue that such a seemingly innocent statement is potentially an unqualified enigma that allows for an infinite play of diverse interpretations. Consider Jacques Derrida's comment on the statement "I have forgotten my umbrella" as recorded

---

[50]Ibid.

[51]Ibid.

[52]Barth, *Church Dogmatics* 2:2, 363.

in the margins of one of Nietzsche's notebooks: "It is always possible that [this phrase] means nothing at all or that it has no decidable meaning. There is no end to its parodying play with meaning. . . . The hermeneut cannot but be provoked and disconcerted by its play."[53] Derrida uses Nietzsche's comment about the forgotten umbrella as a paradigm for the work of language as such: all discourse is characterized by *différance*, that is, language's unnerving capacity to suspend reference to a central object or meaning by unwinding a string of indeterminate significations along an endless line of signifiers. *Différance* is now the recognized fate of all literary texts—texts that are not closed books but open intertexts caught up in an endless play of signs and significations, texts that are endlessly "different" and that "defer" identifying any stable meaning that might ground their playful indeterminacy. Text interpretation is always played out in a "void" or "open space" or "bottomless chessboard" so that "writing literally means nothing. . . . To risk meaning nothing is to start to play, and first to enter into the play of *différance* which prevents any word, any concept, any major enunciation from coming to summarize and to govern from the theological presence of a center the movement and textual spacing of differences."[54]

Barth, on the other hand, would contend that the Old Testament *is* organized (though never controlled) by "the theological presence of a center," to use Derrida's phrase, because of the text's sometimes explicit and sometimes implicit allusion to the Word of God in Jesus Christ. While he recognizes the deconstructionist "open void" option in Leviticus 16, he maintains that if the text is going to be meaningfully retrievable it must be theologically decoded as aimed at something else. And in light of the New Testament, this "something else" can only be Jesus Christ. Of course, Derrida would not disagree with Barth that the text *could* refer to Christ, but he would note that this referent is only one among a plurality of referents, none of which would have priority over any other. Barth, finally, would insist on a christological closure to the interpretative process within the double-meaning (literal and typological) capacities of the Old Testament texts.

In reading Leviticus 16 general hermeneutics cannot help us—only a special hermeneutic informed by the Spirit and undertaken by the imaginative exegete can arrive at this text's christological subject matter. The "older Christian exegesis" was correct in its final judgment that this passage makes sense in light of Christ's sacrificial death, but generally wrong in its procedure for arriving at this conclusion. Interpreting Leviticus ty-

---

[53]Jacques Derrida, *Spurs: Nietzsche's Styles*, trans. Barbara Harlow (Chicago: University of Chicago Press, 1979) 131.

[54]Jacques Derrida, *Positions*, trans. Alan Bass (Chicago: University of Chicago Press, 1981) 14.

pologically cannot be set forth mechanically according to a formula, but given the presupposition of faith, precritical allegorical exegesis is vindicated as legitimate, indeed necessary. "Only the positive decision of faith in Jesus Christ (as the only way really to know him as the One he is) can vindicate the older Christian exegesis of these texts as prophecies of Christ. But by the positive decision of faith that excludes unbelief, this exegesis is rendered not merely possible but even necessary. *How can we believe in Jesus Christ and not of necessity recognize him in these passages?* [Barth's emphasis]"[55] If the hermeneut maintains existential fidelity to the object of her personal faith, then she will discover Christ in the Old Testament—even at the center of ancient (and seemingly opaque) rituals like the Day of Atonement in Leviticus 16. By risking figural readings of the Jewish Bible's characters and incidents as tropes of the New Testament, Israel's stories of election will then be seen as a "type" of Christ—the original and exemplary rejected and elected individual who is the "open secret of the reality of the slain and living man which so utterly transcends the reality of the Old Testament man or of man in general."[56]

As another case of Barth's theological-literary hermeneutic, let us look at his reading of the typological relationship between Judas and Paul in *Church Dogmatics* 2:2. In the Gospels and the Acts of the Apostles, Judas's handing over Jesus to the Gentiles for death typologically anticipates Paul's handing over Jesus to the Gentiles for life. Paul is Judas's antitype: as Judas begins the ministry, as it were, of delivering Jesus over to his enemies, so Paul completes what Judas began in his missionary labors in the hostile Roman world. A careful reading of the complex narrative structure of the Gospels and Acts will uncover Paul's role as an evangelistic continuation and reparation of Judas's initial work (which had begun so badly).

> Paul sets out from the very place where the penitent Judas had tried to turn back and reverse what had already happened. He begins by doing what to Judas' horror the high priests and elders had done as the second links in that chain of evil. He fulfills the handing-over of Jesus to the Gentiles: not this time in unfaithfulness, but in faithfulness to Israel's calling and mission; not now aiming at the slaying of Jesus, but at establishing in the whole world the lordship of this One who was slain but is risen. Judas . . . begins the true story of the apostles in the sense of Mt. 28:19, the genuine handing-over of Jesus to the Gentiles.[57]

---

[55]*Church Dogmatics* 2:1, 364. Barth's vindication of ancient and Reformation hermeneutics of the Old Testament further indicates the misapplication of Smend's label of "postcritical exegesis" with reference to Barth. Again, Barth is not postcritical but metacritical in his strong reading of the whole biblical witness as a figural type of Christ.

[56]Ibid., 365.

[57]Ibid.

Could it be that Paul "fulfills the handing-over of Jesus to the Gentiles" begun by Judas? That while Matthias in Acts 1 is the de jure replacement of Judas, Paul is his de facto replacement? That Paul's self-description as the "least of the apostles" (1 Cor. 15:9) is a subtle, even ironical, reference to his negative kinship with Judas, a kinship to the one who, like himself, was criticized and hated for doing what he deemed best at the time, handing over Jesus and his mission to his enemies, the Gentiles?

Barth freely admits that the "discovery" of this provocative typology may not, in fact, be true to the intentions of the writers of the Gospels and Acts: "We can hardly deny that it is really Paul who took over Judas' place and the work abandoned by him, [yet] whether the Acts of the Apostles really intended to say this implicitly is another question."[58] Again, however, Barth's concern is less with what the text might have meant authorially and originally and more with what it can mean in the present as a work of theological art—as an ingenuous literary whole with complicated compositional devices that set free profound insights into the nature of the biblical God and God's dealings with humankind. As with historical criticism, Barth uses theological-literary criticism to see what insights are yielded by a hermeneutic of the Bible's subject matter. In the Judas/Paul typology, Scripture yields the theological insight that God's ways are not our ways, that God can and often does use the marginalized and rejected among us (in this case Judas) to inaugurate the divine master plan for our salvation (a plan carried through by Paul, the least of the apostles). The ground is level at the foot of the cross: God in Christ may use any of us, even the most despised and hated and traitorous among us, to accomplish the divine will.

At first glance, it is hard to imagine any commonalities between Barth's neo-Reformation *Church Dogmatics*, Northrop Frye's New Critical *The Great Code*, and Mark Taylor's deconstructionist *Erring*. Yet there are such commonalities, at least initially, in each figure's tenacious avoidance of the "genetic" and "authorial intention" fallacies so common to traditional biblical criticism—the reduction of the Bible's meaning as an intertextual whole to the sum of its historical and biographical parts and antecedents. What the Bible does mean in its totality is, of course, hotly disputed by each of these authors. However, Barth and today's disparate proponents of the literary method in theological and biblical studies agree that the Bible's meaning is not an epiphenomenon of background factors. On one level, then, Barth does share a common concern with contemporary literary theorists who read the Bible as a rich, intertextual fabric composed of diverse threads of meaning. Barth's adroit handling of the Judas/Paul typology would be understood today by practitioners of the literary study of the Bible because of its display of the consummate artistry at work in

---

[58]Ibid.

the depiction of this startling relationship between Judas and Paul in the Gospels and Acts.

Be this as it may, it must still be underscored that Barth's hermeneutic, however sophisticated in its literary acumen, is nevertheless in the service of a theological interpretation of the Bible as the church's Scripture. As with historical criticism, he would view literary criticism as a propaedeutic to a theological hermeneutic. As Barth questioned the "historicist" assumption implicit in the historical method of his time, so he would probably question the "textualist" assumption at work in today's literary methods, namely that the exposition of the Bible's internal allusions, literary contrivances, and verbal intricacies is what the study of the Bible is all about. Such a program may be fine for the adequate interpretation of Shakespeare or Brecht, but by itself it is inadequate with reference to the Bible because it cannot account for the Bible's own self-understanding, its claim to be a witness to the Word of God.[59] For Barth, the storied world of the Bible is not simply one world amidst a plurality of other literary worlds; as the Word of God written, it is the divinely chosen textual environment within which God in Christ through the Spirit is actively at play and present to the reader today.

This is a stark and significant difference between Barth and his literary counterparts. For Northrop Frye, for example, the medium *is* the message in biblical interpretation. Marshaling the resources of the New Critical poetics outlined in his landmark *Anatomy of Criticism*, Frye in *The Great Code* argues that the Bible is a self-referential, poetic text that makes no claims on describing external reality. Its meaning is centripetal, not centrifugal; it is the words within the Bible, not the events referred to by these words, that constitute the "mythological universe" that is the Bible.[60] The biblical stories are fiction for their own sake, not history for the sake of describing the external world; they are poetically evocative, even existentially meaningful, but they are not mimetically transparent upon historical reality as such. Because the Bible is a poetic, not a descriptive text, the "realities" of which it speaks only "exist" within their own textual world and not outside of it in observable history. Indeed, the divine life itself is not an external reality outside of the text but a function of the Bible's poetic universe: "We could almost say that even the existence of God is an inference from the existence of the Bible: in the *beginning* was the Word."[61] Because the Bible as poetry suspends its referential aspect, Jesus Christ, like God, has the same text-bound status as a metaphorical reality specific

---

[59]See ibid., 1:2, 483-500.

[60]Northrop Frye, *The Great Code: The Bible and Literature* (New York: Harcourt Brace Jovanovich, 1981) xi-xxiii.

[61]Ibid., 61.

to the self-contained, centripetal world of the Bible. The biblical hero "Jesus Christ" is literarily equivalent to the Bible itself as the fully human, fully divine Word of God: "From this point of view it makes good sense to call the Bible and the person of Christ by the same name."[62]

Frye's separation of the world of the text and the world outside the text is consistent with recent deconstructionist readings of Scripture. For Mark C. Taylor, there is nothing beyond the Bible's literary world, no "transcendental signified" that can either fix the meaning of the biblical texts or to which these texts can give us access. For the theological Derrideans, the Bible is a melange of free-floating signs—signs that are signs of other signs—none of which can be secured by any independently signified reality outside the text. "Since there is no transcendental signified to anchor the activity of signification, freely floating signs cannot be tied down to any single meaning. Everything in the divine milieu is thoroughly transitional and radically relative."[63] Beyond its figural world, there is no extratextual reality that can fix the meaning of Scripture amidst the constant intersecting and interplaying of the biblical texts. Without any Logos behind the veil of signs, with no absolute to secure the meaning of the text, deconstructionism emerges as the only viable postmodern theological option after the death of God. "In view of its remarkable grasp of the far-reaching significance of the dissolution of the Western theological and philosophical tradition, it would not be too much to suggest that *deconstructionism is the 'hermeneutic' of the death of God.*"[64] Taylor's affirmation of Nietzsche's haunting verdict on religion—that God has died and we have killed him—gives his postmodernist reading of the biblical heritage a more radical cast than that offered by modernist New Critical theorists like Frye. Yet both men share the same basic assumption: the Bible, like any other classic literary document, is a plurality of oscillating intertexts without a stable extralinguistic referent to ground its meaning.

Such an assumption could not be further from the intent of Barth's hermeneutic. While the Swiss theologian, along with Frye and Taylor, does celebrate the play of meaning in the Bible—his free use of the scapegoat/Jesus Christ and Judas/Paul typologies are only two of many examples—he would disavow what I have labeled the "textualist" assumption, that textual meaning is always radically open and indeterminate. Barth celebrates play, yes, but not ceaseless play that dogmatically is opposed to the always surprising entrance of a divine Other into the interpretive game, an Other who might center the play and direct it along a deter-

---

[62]Ibid., 77.

[63]Mark C. Taylor, *Erring: A Postmodern A/theology* (Chicago: University of Chicago Press, 1984) 16.

[64]Ibid., 6.

minate course. Barth would agree that the text is deep, but not so deep that to follow its meaning is to enter into a serpentine abyss with no sure footholds, no reasonable steps one might take given the steps others have taken in their encounters with this Other.

Taylor would undoubtedly label Barth's penchant for an Other to center the interpretive process to be a self-indicting variation on the regnant forms of "logocentrism" that have always characterized Western theology and metaphysics. But Barth was always quick to point out that the biblical texts do not *possess* an immediate and determinate meaning that is lying there in the text, raw and ready and waiting for any interpreter to extract. Barth's concern to hear the Word in the words of the Bible does not mean that he stubbornly expects to find a static Logos, a fully self-present Other within Scripture that can be used to shut down and control the playful freedom, the give-and-take between text and interpreter, that constitutes all hermeneutical understanding. Though the Bible is not totally unstable as radically acentric *différance,* it does contain an open number of *differences* as a now unified, now intertextual plenitude of meaning.[65] The Bible is an open and diffuse intertext, but its meaning is not forever played out on a "bottomless chessboard" with no boundaries, no limitations, no rough approximations one might make as to its more or less determinate meaning. Though open to the play of meaning in the biblical texts Barth's hermeneutic, in its controlling interest to allow God to speak in these texts through the witness of the Spirit, is a radical departure from current literary critics' basic presuppositions. Barth's theological hermeneutic risks the belief that the Bible, as the church's Scripture, does have a relatively stable though never fully determinate and self-present extra-historical and extralinguistic referent, the referent of the divine life itself as that life encounters the reader whenever and wherever it is graciously disposed to do so.

• Conclusion •

Barth's overarching theological concern is to understand the Bible as something more than a finely crafted literary text or historically determined cultural artifact. Instead, the Bible should be read on its own terms as a living theological voice. Its literary intricacies and historical antecedents are not to be studied as ends in themselves but as means to the end that the divine life itself might be revealed to the interpreter of these texts under the aegis and guidance of the Holy Spirit. Nevertheless, there is no hermeneutical guarantee that can assure the reader that she has accurately conveyed the spirit and intent of the biblical message in her inter-

---

[65]For Taylor, see *Erring,* chaps. 4 and 8; for Derrida, see "Différance," in his *Margins of Philosophy,* trans. Alan Bass (Chicago: University of Chicago Press, 1982) 1-28.

pretation. Indeed, it is only the promise of the Spirit's presence in the interpretative process that can make possible the true conveyance of the Bible's subject matter. "Hence one cannot lay down conditions which, if observed, guarantee hearing of the Word. . . . There is nothing of this kind because God's Word is a mystery in the sense that it truly strikes us spiritually, i.e., in all circumstances only through the Holy Spirit, in all its indirectness only directly from God."[66] A virtuoso aptitude for exposing the Bible's word plays and images, or a rigorous historical examination of its Near Eastern sources, is hermeneutically impotent if not explicitly joined to the patient, Spirit-guided listening for the Word in the words of the biblical texts.

Barth's notion of the role of the Holy Spirit in the work of interpretation marks one of the novel advances of his hermeneutic beyond the dominant models for exegesis in his time and ours. Not that Barth's hermeneutic is historically new in this regard: Calvin, for example, had argued that the Holy Spirit is the "inner teacher" who effectually illumines what we read and hear in the Bible to be God's Word.[67] Yet it is to Barth's credit that he adapted Calvin's insight for post-Enlightenment scholarship by arguing that an insular historical or literary approach cannot account for the necessary "pneumatic" moment in the interpretive process.

There is an obvious danger, however, in a contemporary reappropriation of Barth's method. Has not the work of the Holy Spirit too often been invoked in biblicist exegesis as the guarantor of the Bible's divine character in opposition to its human origins? It has, certainly, but a docetic hermeneutic is not what is being suggested here. Rather, the model proposed views critical biblical studies as a necessary and integral part of an overarching theological hermeneutic—a hermeneutic that uses the insights of the historian and the literary critic to support the theological expectation that the divine life might somehow be heard again through the scriptural texts. All three moments—historical, literary, and theological—are needed for the development of a sustained hermeneutic that is critically attuned to the biblical words and that is spiritually sensitive to a possible Word within these words. Within this framework, the interpreter approaches the text with the hope that the inwardly mysterious work of the Spirit might enable what has been studied historically and literarily to become for the reader the promise of new life, the promise of salvation.

Any historical or literary hermeneutic of the Bible that is opposed to its claim to be the Word of God, to be Scripture, is fundamentally flawed because it does not tally with the Bible's historic intent to be the textual

---

[66]Barth, *Church Dogmatics* 1:1, 183.

[67]John Calvin, *Institutes of the Christian Religion,* ed. John T. McNeill, trans. Ford Lewis Battles, 2 vols. (Philadelphia: Westminster Press, 1960) 1:537-42.

mediation of God's Word to the human community. This does not mean that the interpreter must be a religious believer. It is rather that without the operative assumption that these texts are potential kerygma, the Bible remains simply a partisan historical record or a great piece of literature—nothing more. I may not have been convinced by what it says, yet its claim to be written revelation should still be respected in its own right as worthy of my hermeneutical attention. For whenever this claim is not respected, the provocative power and depth of the Bible's message is not adequately sounded and explored. Reading the Bible demands something like the rigorous "thick description" Clifford Geertz uses in his interpretation of culture: allowing the text at hand—be it written on paper or culturally inscribed—to signify a world of meanings that cannot be explained by, or reduced to, the various historical and structural factors that were at work in the text's formation.[68]

While traditional historical criticism is helpful in isolating the formative events that gave rise to the biblical message, it can exceed its limits by assuming that this excavative work is what the interpretation of the Bible is all about. And while modern and postmodern literary criticism elucidates the delicate verbal patterns and sophisticated plot structures that make up the Bible's text-world, its antireferential bias can render it oblivious to the possibility that the text might have the power to mediate to the reader the life and presence of the divine Other in the hermeneutical process. A Barthlike hermeneutic that highlights the Bible's claim to be the Word of God written suggests that an isolated historical or literary study of the Bible fails by refusing to allow the Bible to be something more than the sum total of its historical parts or a self-contained literary world. A theological hermeneutic, on the other hand, that combines and deepens the insights of the historical and critical methods will seek to develop these insights as an aid to rediscovering the biblical texts as a living voice through which the Word of God can be heard again in a "new naiveté," as Jüngel writes, for the modern reader.

---

[68]Clifford Geertz, "Thick Description: Toward an Interpretive Theory of Culture," in his *The Interpretation of Cultures* (New York: Basic Books, 1973) 3-30.

THEOLOGICAL HERMENEUTICS AND PAUL RICOEUR

Yet, it is in terms of one certain presupposition that I stand in the position of a listener to Christian preaching. I assume that this speaking is meaningful, that it is worthy of consideration, and that examining it may accompany and guide the transfer from the text to life where it will verify itself fully.

Can I account for this presupposition? Alas, I stumble already. I do not know how to sort out what is here "unravelable" situation, uncriticized custom, deliberate preference, or profound choice. I can only confess that my desire to hear more is all these things, and that it defies all these distinctions.[1]

• The Wager of Faith •

Ricoeur's religious thought begins with the wager that there is something of crucial importance to be interpreted in the fullness of biblical language. It begins with the "assumption that this kind of discourse is not senseless, that it is worthwhile to analyze it, because something is said that is not said by other kinds of discourse."[2] This wager is made uneasily, however, because Ricoeur maintains that the God of the Bible cannot be theoretically proven as a staple of reason or as a fact alongside other facts in our empirical experience. Ricoeur has absorbed Kant's critique against any natural theology that would try to prove the existence of God by an appeal to the necessities of thought or the knowledge of empirical objects. Ricoeur's wager "relies on signs, not proofs,"[3] as he puts it; it re-

---

[1]Paul Ricoeur, "Naming God," *Union Seminary Quarterly Review* 34 (1979): 215.

[2]Paul Ricoeur, "Philosophy and Religious Language," *Journal of Religion* 54 (1974): 71.

[3]Paul Ricoeur, "Hope and the Structure of Philosophical Systems," *Proceedings of the American Catholic Philosophical Association* 44 (1970): 59.

lies on the signs or "traces" of a reality testified to at the horizon of philosophical reflection that demands to be interpreted and understood. At the boundaries of philosophical discourse, he finds that the scriptural witness to the presence of the absolute in history compels us to risk an interpretation of this witness because it "operates in such a way that we do not dispose of this language, but this is a language which disposes of us."[4]

The interpretation of this language "which disposes of us" has the status of a wager: it may be the case that a lie exists in the heart of the witnessing community that would result in false testimony.[5] But the risk must be taken because the stakes are so high—the stakes being the possibility of biblical language being a faithful trace of God's presence in the Jewish and Christian communities. In principle, however, there can be no neutral or apodictic warrant for settling whether the absolute does or does not disclose itself in the biblical witness. Countering Hegel, Ricoeur believes that knowledge of the absolute is never given in an absolute sense but only relative to the contingent and fallible signs that the divine life gives of itself in its generosity. "Compared to the scientific ideal which constitutes [absolute knowledge], hermeneutics of testimony appears to be blemished by relativity."[6] Ricoeur ventures the Kantian "hope" (without Hegel's certitude) that the church's sacred texts are an authentic testimony to the presence of the absolute in history.[7] This hope arises from the ashes of reason's misguided attempt to prove the existence of God on the basis of our objective knowledge; it is a hope that has a precarious existence on the boundaries of reason's need to know what cannot be made rationally obvious or empirically certain. It is probable (but never certain) that God has spoken through the biblical witness, though

> [t]here is no apodictic form of a response to the recurring question: how do we assure ourselves that the affirmation is not arbitrary, that God is not constructed, almost picked, from certain testimonies that other consciousnesses could contest, since there indeed is no fact which can be dissociated from the idea which gives meaning to it, a meaning that transcends the fact itself.[8]

---

[4]Paul Ricoeur, "The Language of Faith," in *The Philosophy of Paul Ricoeur: An Anthology of His Work*, ed. Charles E. Regan (Boston: Beacon Press, 1978) 233.

[5]Paul Ricoeur, "The Hermeneutics of Testimony," in *Essays on Biblical Interpretation*, ed. Lewis S. Mudge (Philadelphia: Fortress Press, 1980) 128-29.

[6]Ibid., 149.

[7]Ricoeur, "Hope," 67; see also idem, "Freedom in the Light of Hope," in *Essays on Biblical Interpretation*, 155-82.

[8]Ricoeur, "Hermeneutics of Testimony," 150.

The biblical God is that "eruption of something from the other side"[9] that erects a radical discontinuity between our systematic thought and the Other's disorienting particularity. A theological hermeneutic can only attest to this eruption in history; it cannot prove that it happened. As confessional as this may sound, the final warrant for Ricoeur's wager of faith is nothing other than the "extraordinarily fragile testimony" given of the absolute by the witnessing church. "This means that the Gospel will always be carried by an extraordinarily fragile testimony, that of the preacher, that of personal life, that of community. There is no proof which can support either the experience or the rationale. In this sense, the Cross *remains* a folly for the intelligent, a scandal for the wise."[10]

Thought does not operate in a void because it always starts from the givens of language, culture, and history. As we noted with reference to Gadamer's hermeneutic, understanding always operates within the horizon of our presuppositional "foreunderstandings" or "prejudices." Gadamer's argument in his masterful *Truth and Method* is that *productive* prejudices enable the interpreter to pursue openly the task of inquiry and understanding. Moreover, his recognition of the power of our pre-grasp of the world to enable our understanding of it criticizes the Cartesian and Enlightenment ideal of tradition-free, presuppositionless explanations of reality through clear and distinct ideas.[11] Gadamer provocatively avers that it is our prejudices, not our enlightened judgments, that enable our openness to the world: the process of knowing cannot begin without our tacit assumptions about the nature of things. Ricoeur's hermeneutic appropriates this Gadamerian insight. He considers the project dear to much of modern philosophy—that is, beginning thought without any preferences—illusory due to the inevitable interlocking of thought with our prior experiences and fundamental choices. Theological reflection is no exception to the rule that human knowing is a fiduciary process constituted by our founding biases toward the world.

In the Christian tradition, the bias that has the status of "acquired authority" is that God has been adequately identified or "named" in the biblical texts. "Naming God only comes about within the milieu of a presupposition, incapable of being rendered transparent to itself, suspected of being a vicious circle, and tormented by contingency. This is the presupposition: Naming God is what has already taken place in the texts

---

[9]Ricoeur, "The Critique of Religion," in *Philosophy of Paul Ricoeur*, 219.

[10]Ibid., 220. See also the criticism of Ricoeur's preference for the biblical witness in his theological hermeneutic in David E. Klemm, *The Hermeneutical Theory of Paul Ricoeur* (Lewisburg PA: Bucknell University Press, 1983).

[11]Hans-Georg Gadamer, *Truth and Method*, trans. Garret Barden and John Cumming (New York: Continuum Press, 1975) 235-58.

preferred by my listening's presupposition."[12] This presupposition is un-abashedly intrabiblical: it cannot be demonstrated as valid outside the cir-cle of Christian faith by extratheological resources. But while the other disciplines cannot adjudicate the presuppositional claims of the Christian tradition to "name God," they can be used to explicate the distinctive content of faith by presuming (however tentatively) the power of the bib-lical witness to illumine and transform human experience. In borrowing insights from contemporary philosophy of language in particular, the goal of Ricoeur's hermeneutic is to provide occasions for the God who is named in the Bible to be experienced again in contemporary communities of in-terpretation.

• The Use of Discourse Analysis •

Ricoeur's theological hermeneutic seeks to provide the methodologi-cal guidelines for interpreting the biblical words as an occasion for the Word of God. Because it is the "words" as an instance of the "Word" that are being interpreted, his model is a thoroughgoing exercise in the un-derstanding of language as such and therefore is placed at the intersec-tion between general issues in linguistics, philosophy of language, and general hermeneutics on the one hand, and the particular interests of bib-lical exegesis within the Christian community of faith, on the other. Theological hermeneutics is an exercise in the interpretation of meaning in language, but it is the meaning given in the distinctive language of the biblical witness that is its proper and particular object of inquiry. General hermeneutical insights can assist the understanding of the Word in the words for a theological interpretation theory; hence, the Christian her-meneut must place the problems of interpretation per se at the heart of her concerns because the understanding of the unique object of theolog-ical hermeneutics, the Word of God, refracts the issues raised in general hermeneutics.

Ricoeur's clearest programmatic exposition of his theological herme-neutic is found in "Contribution d'une réflexion sur le langage à une théologie de la parole" where he highlights the need to correlate general linguistic issues with the special language reality of the Word of God given in the biblical texts and church proclamation.

> 1. All the affirmations of theologians rest on the conviction that God meets man as discourse; we speak of the "Word of God."
> 2. Christianity is, in its primary designation, the comprehension of this Word insofar as it "becomes flesh."
> 3. The testimony of the first Christian community constitutes a form of discourse, the Word of preaching, as the place where the event of Christ had identified itself as word.

---

[12]Ricoeur, "Naming God," 215.

4. Present-day preaching is in its way the actualization of this first word, primarily in a new Word intelligible for our times.

5. The work of exegetes and of theologians is in its way a sort of discourse on these four successive discourses, with the ultimate end of recovering and reaffirming the meaning of the original Word which places in movement this continuation of words.[13]

This passage records Ricoeur's clearest definition to date of the task of theology as a hermeneutic of the Word of God. Theology is the interpretation of the original Word of God as it has been mediated through the incarnate Word of Christ, the primitive testimony to the Christ event in the early church, and, finally, the proclamation of the gospel in the present. "All theology is a theology of the Word,"[14] Ricoeur says, because all theology is a sustained interpretation of the proclamation of the divine Word under a historical succession of different forms of discourse. The inaugural Word of God sets in motion the dynamic succession of subsequent discourses on this inaugural Word; the corresponding task of a theological hermeneutic is to understand this originating Word as a new Word of power for the modern situation. For Ricoeur, then, theology is linguistic in origin, kerygmatic in subject matter, and hermeneutical in method: theology is the interpretation of the biblical words as traces of the Word of God as that Word has been presented through consecutive historical mediations.

For Ricoeur, it is precisely because the Word of God is an event of our everyday language that a productive relationship between a theology of the Word and philosophy of language can be established. "That the logos would become discourse, that would be elevated to the rank of our *words*, this is that *event* that creates the meeting between the theology of the Word and linguistic studies."[15] Here Ricoeur alludes to the role of "discourse"

---

[13]Paul Ricoeur, "Contribution d'une réflexion sur le language à une théologie de la parole" in *Exégèse et Herméneutique: Parole de Dieu*, ed. Xavier Léon-Dufour (Paris: Editions du Seuil, 1971) 301-20 [my translation of this passage and all subsequent references to this article].

[14]Ibid., 302. Ricoeur's comments in "théologie de la parole" concerning the exigency to correlate a theology of the Word and linguistic studies make clear his indebtedness to many of the signal insights of the New Hermeneutic movement in Germany and America in the postwar period. But his own position is more than a gloss on, or even an extension of, the issues raised in the New Hermeneutic debates. As a philosopher of language, his ability to marshal the resources within contemporary philosophical hermeneutics for his own biblical interpretations explicitly shifts the level of discussion concerning theological hermeneutics onto a more philosophically sophisticated and interdisciplinary plane than had hitherto been the case.

[15]Ricoeur, "théologie de la parole," 303.

in forging a mediation between the study of language and a theology of the Word of God. Ricoeur's theory of discourse sets forth the principles that guide his integration of general language studies and the special language of the Word, so that understanding his theory of discourse is the key to understanding the relationship between his theological hermeneutic and his overall hermeneutical philosophy. Ricoeur's conception of *how* the word-event of Christian witness functions is situated within his understanding of the dynamics of language (as discourse) in general. In this section I will examine Ricoeur's language philosophy in order to expand our understanding of his theological hermeneutic as a variation on his theory of discourse.

Ricoeur's notion of "discourse" emphasizes the nature of language as a speech-event with the capacity to refer to reality and not simply to the discrete linguistic units (like phonemes and morphemes) that underlie language. "I take discourse to mean the actualization of language in a speech-event based on a kind of unit irreducible to the constituents of language as 'code.' This basic unit of language as speech or discourse is the sentence."[16] Language on the level of the sentence can be said to refer to extralinguistic reality beyond the self-contained world of semiotic codes. Language is not a formal dictionary of individual words and meaning units that only refer to other words and units within the lexical system; rather, language as discourse is constituted of sentences that open out onto the world.

All discourse contains three characteristics: first, a speaker; second, a reference; third, an audience. "Language or discourse has a speaker, a world, and a vis-à-vis. These three traits together constitute discourse as an 'event' in a three-fold sense: the speaker is brought to language; a dimension of the world is brought to language; and a dialogue between human beings is brought to language."[17] Ricoeur maintains that in the vis-à-vis between speaker and audience, features of the world are opened up through the miracle of shared meaning. In the give-and-take of discourse, what is private to the speaker ("utterer's meaning") is now made public to an audience ("utterance meaning") through the structured, internal conventions of meaning characteristic of all discourse that seeks to say something about the external world.

What is at stake, then, in Ricoeur's theory of discourse is the preservation of language's ability to refer to reality. Signs refer to other signs within a semiotic system, but language as discourse refers beyond itself to the world.

The referential character of discourse is structured either under the conditions of writing or speaking. In oral discourse reference is osten-

---

[16]Paul Ricoeur, "Biblical Hermeneutics," *Semeia* 4 (1975): 66.
[17]Ibid.

sive: the thing referred to in spoken language can always be identified through gesture; the use of demonstratives, adverbs, and verbal tenses; and, most important, through the to-and-fro of dialogue between speaker and listener. If I do not understand what you are saying (or what you intended to say), I can ask for clarification and you can repeat what you have said and/or "point" to the object in question (be it ideal or real) in order to clarify what you meant.

Written discourse, however, supersedes the dialogical encounter and reference is no longer as easy as identifying what was said or intended in a given, here-and-now situation. In fact, the mental intention of the speaker (now author) is no longer accessible in the written environment because the hearer (now reader) cannot ask the speaker (now author) what was meant by a particular statement or statements. Written discourse, therefore, witnesses the disassociation between authorial intention and textual meaning because discourse that was once under the control of the question-and-answer situation is now textual discourse, structured under the conditions of diverse forms of literary production (i.e., composition, genre, and style) and subject to a conflict of interpretations based on the open number of readers at any given time.

Ricoeur maintains that a text is structured according to rules of overall synthesis (composition), formal modes of expression (genre), and identifiable characteristics of literary individuality (style). These features of written discourse give rule-governed shape and form to an author's intentions, making a text a *work* of public discourse rather than a private *extension* of an author's interior life. Composition, genre, and style make a literary expression available for wider consumption; though the "saying" of discourse passes in speech, the "said" of discourse as public meaning perdures. Thus, Ricoeur's formula is: "If all discourse is actualized as an event, all discourse is understood as meaning."[18] What lasts is not the original author's intention but the propositional meaning or "ideality" of discourse that is "fixed" by means of the codified rules of language that produce the text as a work of discourse. These formal features of discourse—composition, genre, and style—produce the text as a public work because they bring about a text's "semantic autonomy" from its author and objectively "mark" the text as a work of communication and controversy. Now any competent reader can enter the interpretive fray and question the text's meaning on the basis of its publicly available semantic structure.[19]

---

[18]Paul Ricoeur, *Interpretation Theory: Discourse and the Surplus of Meaning* (Fort Worth: Texas Christian University Press, 1976) 12.

[19]Ibid., 34-37. David Tracy clearly explains the role of "ideal meaning" in Ricoeur's interpretation theory: "The meaning or intention of the text is now available not merely to the original conversation partner (who may or may not have

Hermeneutics seek to adjudicate this conflict of interpretations based on a particular reading's fidelity to the text's immanent sense and intended reference, that is, its meaning. Because the text is now separated from its original situation and the author's intentions, it enters the public domain of many readers and many interpretations. Yet while the text is autonomous, it is not an "authorless entity," as Ricoeur says.[20] Written discourse follows a movement in which something is said by someone to someone about something; in this movement, an author's intentions always pass over into the text's formal, literary structure. Once this "passing over" from speaking to writing has occurred, the mental intention of the author can no longer be ostensively inquired about because the original speaking situation no longer obtains. Hence, the goal of interpretation becomes not inquiring into what the text "meant" (an impossibility given the text's semantic autonomy) but into what the text "means" (a possibility given the text's public character as a work of discourse).

Here Ricoeur's indebtedness to formalist-structuralist linguistics is apparent. He agrees with the New Critics, like William K. Wimsatt, Jr., who argue against the so-called "intentional fallacy, which holds the author's intention as the only valid criterion for any valid interpretation of the text."[21] Ricoeur believes with the structuralists and the New Critics

---

properly understood it) but rather to anyone who can read. In his theory of interpretation, the concept of meaning is the Husserlian one adapted by Paul Ricoeur: meaning is neither psychic nor a physical event but is *ideal* or *noematic*. As ideal and as fixed in written texts or in oral modes of discourse, the meaning undergoes a process of distanciation from the author's intention, from the original dialogue situation, and from its first audience. At the same time, the meaning is now available in these texts for any intelligent interpreter to understand upon reading them" (David Tracy, *Blessed Rage for Order: The New Pluralism in Theology* [New York: Seabury Press, 1975] 75).

[20]Ricoeur, *Interpretation Theory*, 30.

[21]Ibid. Wimsatt agrees with Lionel Trilling, T. S. Eliot, and others that it is impossible to "divine" an author's intention in a literary work and, therefore, interpretation should labor to understand the formal "meaning" of the work itself (see William K. Wimsatt and Cleanth Brooks, *Literary Criticism: A Short History*, 2 vols. [Chicago: University of Chicago Press, 1957] 2:546-51, 714-15).

Opposing Ricoeur and the New Critics on the question of authorial intention are those literary theorists and theologians who follow Johann August Ernesti, who held that hermeneutics is the science of uncovering the meaning that a text's author intended. E. D. Hirsch, Jr. has cogently argued for Ernesti's position in this country: "All valid interpretation of every sort is founded on the re-cognition of what an author meant" (E. D. Hirsch, Jr., *Validity in Interpretation* [New Haven CT: Yale University Press, 1967] 126). For a theological appropriation of Ernesti's and Hirsch's position, see Charles M. Wood, *The Formation of Christian Understanding: An Essay in Theological Hermeneutics* (Philadelphia: Fortress Press, 1981) esp. 61-75.

that the meaning of a literary text is autonomous from the mind of its cre-
ator, and, as we will see in his biblical exegesis, Ricoeur welcomes the use
of formalist-structuralist methods to analyze the text's semantic patterns.
But Ricoeur has always been careful to distinguish between "structural
analysis as the science of structures and structuralism as the ideology of
absolute texts [*ideologie du texte en soi*]."[22] While structuralism (as structural analysis) has rightly recognized that a text escapes the finitude of its
author, structuralism (as structuralist ideology) cannot account for the
creation of new meaning in discourse beyond the bounds of a text's semiotic codes. Reaching beyond structuralist ideology, Ricoeur introduces
the Benvenistian notion of discourse so that a text can be recognized as
an event with the power of extralinguistic reference, even though a text,
as written discourse, cannot refer situationally and ostensively. Ricoeur
says that, thanks to writing, readers can now experience a whole "world"
of possible meanings in the text beyond the dialogical "situation" of spoken discourse. "This first extension of the scope of reference beyond the
narrow boundaries of the dialogical situation is of tremendous conse-
quence. Thanks to writing, man and only man has a world and not just
a situation. . . . In the same manner that the text frees its meaning from
the tutelage of the mental intention, it frees its reference from the limits
of situational reference. For us, the world is the ensemble of references
opened up by the text."[23]

Now that the general category of discourse has been specified in Ricoeur's thought, we can ask the question as to the relationship between
this category and his theological hermeneutic. The power of biblical language to transcend its original speech situation through written discourse is accomplished by the rich variety of literary genres or modes of
discourse within which the faith of Israel and the early church was first
inscribed. The theological vision embodied in the biblical texts is modulated by the Bible's diverse forms of discourse, such as narration, legis-
lation, prophecy, history, wisdom, hymns, and prayers. Though biblical
exegetes and literary critics have long noted the presence of these diverse
genres within the Bible, what is significant about Ricoeur's hermeneutic
is his argument that these various modes of discourse are means of literary *production* in which different facets of the divine revealing are actually generated through the use of these forms. Revelation, then, is
coextensive with the varieties of discourse characteristic of the biblical
texts.[24]

The Bible's modes of discourse are not mere classificatory devices that,
upon identification, can be set aside as unrelated to the text's message:

---

[22]Ricoeur, "théologie de la parole," 287.

[23]Ricoeur, *Interpretation Theory*, 36.

[24]Ricoeur, "Philosophy and Religious Language," 73-75.

"The literary genres of the Bible do not constitute a rhetorical facade which it would be possible to pull down in order to reveal some thought content that is indifferent to its literary vehicle."[25] Rather, these genres as modes of discourse are theologically significant as the means by which biblical discourse is produced as a *work*—as a network of interconnecting theologies that are fundamentally shaped by the forms of articulation characteristic of each of these theologies' sometimes shared, and sometimes very different, visions of reality. Ricoeur's position that the Bible's varied forms of discourse have a productive function evokes an image of the Bible as a kind of vehicle that moves forward whenever its gears are engaged, and they mesh with the wheels that turn its engine. The Bible's linguistic forms are like so many intermeshing gears that generate its movement as a work of meaningful discourse. In observing some of the primary expressions of this interlocking between theological content and linguistic form, I will take up here three of the modalities of discourse that Ricoeur identifies as most characteristic of the Old and New Testament: prophecy, wisdom, and narrative.[26]

Prophetic discourse is the basic starting point for comprehending the role of the biblical forms of discourse. This is the discourse of the divine word-event, of kerygmatic announcement, of testimony to the Other, of the event of the Word of God in the community. Insofar as "all theology is a theology of the Word,"[27] prophetic discourse is the inaugural discourse that constitutes Israel's faith, as well as that of the early church. It includes two modes of speaking: the forthtelling of the divine message for the people of God, and the foretelling of future events in which God will judge those within and those outside the faithful community. But whether prophetic discourse is of the order of a kerygmatic message to the community, or a disruptive warning concerning God's plans in the end times, it is first and foremost the discourse that bears the stamp of divine authority because it articulates divine intentions for the world and humankind. As the language of prophetic announcement—"Thus says the Lord"—prophetic discourse receives priority in the modalities of biblical language because it mediates the very words of God. "It seems le-

---

[25] Ricoeur, "Toward a Hermeneutic of the Idea of Revelation," in *Essays on Biblical Interpretation*, 91.

[26] In "Hermeneutic of Revelation," and other writings, Ricoeur also speaks of prescriptive and hymnic writings as two other modes of biblical discourse. But because prescriptive discourse for Ricoeur is basically the practical expression of the prophetic Word of God, and because hymnic discourse is essentially the lyrical extension of all other modes of discourse we will consider, I have not explicitly looked at these two genres in the exposition of the other modes of discourse that Ricoeur examines.

[27] Ricoeur, "théologie de la parole," 303.

gitimate to begin by taking prophetic discourse as our basic axis of inquiry. Indeed, this is the discourse which declares itself to be pronounced in the name of . . ."[28]

Ricoeur's initial assignment of priority to prophecy within the plurality of the Bible's modes of discourse is counterbalanced, however, by his argument that a theology of the prophetic Word is too abstract if it does not recognize the nonverbal dimensions of biblical revelation in wisdom discourse, and it is ahistorical if it does not acknowledge the rootedness of revelation in the founding events of Israel's and the church's past. To place the accent in religious discourse solely on the divine word-event is to miss other modalities for the divine disclosure, that is, the critical role of sacred symbols and sacred history in the formation of Israel's and the church's faith. We will consider in Ricoeur's exegesis of Mark's Gospel the role of narrative discourse in his biblical hermeneutics; here, however, we turn to wisdom discourse as the place where the clear affirmation of divine design and intentions in the Word of proclamation is adjusted by the more ambiguous, and sometimes more satisfying, discourse of the divine mystery, even the divine eclipse, which speaks to the boundary situations of human finitude and suffering.

Wisdom discourse gives expression to the symbols of the sacred in nature and the cosmos in contradistinction to the words of the prophets, which battle against these symbols as deficient manifestations of the divine reality. Clearly in the Hebraic domain, Ricoeur argues, the prophetic Word has the upper hand as the voice of judgment against any natural and cosmic sacredness, however diffuse and general. But Ricoeur suggests that the event of the Word of God would be without depth and substance if it did not maintain some resonances to our experiences of hierophany and the numinous within the sacred order. And insofar as revelation is mediated through the Bible's various literary styles and genres, then both the corrective power of the prophetic Word, and the primordial truths embodied within sacred symbols and the sage's wisdom, are needed for a full-orbed presentation of the divine reality.[29] "It should

---

[28]Ricoeur, "Hermeneutic of Revelation," 75.

[29]Ricoeur contends that the biblical world maintains a tension between the proclamation of the Word and the epiphany of the sacred. He acknowledges his indebtedness to Mircea Eliade for recognizing this tension, but his use of Eliade is qualified because he does not sense that the historian of religion fully comprehends the emphasis placed on the Word over against the sacred in the biblical heritage: "In Christianity there is a polarity of proclamation and manifestation, which Mircea Eliade does not recognize in his homogeneous concept of manifestation, epiphany, and so forth. . . . But I think there is something specific in the Hebraic and Christian traditions which gives a kind of privilege to the word" (Paul Ricoeur, "The 'Sacred' Text and the Community," *The Critical Study of Sacred Texts*

also begin to be apparent how the notion of revelation differs from one mode of discourse to another; especially when we pass from prophecy to wisdom. The prophet claims divine inspiration as guaranteeing what he says. The sage does nothing of the sort. He does not declare that his speech is the speech of another. But he does know that wisdom precedes him and that in a way it is through participation in wisdom that someone may be said to be wise."[30]

Wisdom discourse, then, speaks to our fundamental belonging to a sacred order prior to the prophets' judgment against this order; the symbolism embodied in the Hebrew and Christian Scripture's poetic, proverbial, erotic, and hymnic writings both deepens the prophet's message and protects the message from becoming too cerebral. The Judeo-Christian proclamation concerning death and rebirth, for example, would certainly be less meaningful without our primitive experience of the rhythms of the earth in the planting and return of vegetation each year; and the Jewish law concerning circumcision as well as the Christian preaching about baptism would be far less rich if such proclamation were not rooted in our basic experience of spiritual uncleanliness and concomitant need for ablution.

In "Manifestation and Proclamation," Ricoeur presents a program for mediating the dialectic between the preaching of the Word of God and the cosmic disclosure of the sacred. He acknowledges, however, that the main line of the biblical message would not support any such mediation because of the prophets' iconoclastic vigilance to preserve the dominance of the revealed Name over the natural symbol as a hedge against the always-encroaching danger of nature-governed idol worship. "I will say first of all that with the Hebraic faith the word outweighs the numinous . . . the instruction through the Torah outweighs any manifestation through an image."[31] It is understandable why the Hebrew teachers and prophets battled against the potential of nature's symbol-rich elements—such as sky, earth, water—to usurp the role of the verbal Word of God in the community. Without the critical guidance of Torah, Israel would have inevitably slipped back into its earlier role of a tribal cultus unable to carry the universal burden of being God's chosen people for the salvation of humankind.

Yet in spite of the needed stress on the Word versus the numinous in Israel's faith, Ricoeur does not think that the numinous was ever fully

---

[Berkeley: Graduate Theological Union, 1979] 275). This statement is one reason why I will place Ricoeur's hermeneutic closer to Barth's than, say, to Eliade's: the identity of the Christian community rests on its encounter with the divine Word as it is mediated by the community's sacred texts.

[30]Ricoeur, "Hermeneutic of Revelation," 87-88.

[31]Paul Ricoeur, "Manifestation and Proclamation," *Blaisdell Institute Journal* 11 (1978): 21-22.

eclipsed in Israel's experience, or that it should have been. Indeed, it is out of the matrix of the people's encounter with the sacred in the cosmos that Scripture's wisdom and hymnic discourse receives many of its themes and much of its sustaining power. And though these forms of discourse were not given the wide register that the Bible's narrative and prophetic genres were given, they were very much a part of the canon and essential to expressing Israel's common human struggles with life's limitations (death, disease, injustice) and celebrations of life's joys and wonders (birth, prosperity, beauty). Unlike some biblical critics,[32] Ricoeur does not regard the Wisdom writings as a marginal mode of biblical discourse, but as fundamentally indigenous to Israel's and the church's experience of unjust suffering in the face of evil; of confusion vis-à-vis life's complexities; of ineffable wonder at the sight of God's bounty in the created order.

Ricoeur's hermeneutic seeks to give due consideration both to the Bible's theologies of the Word and its recorded experiences of the sacred in spite of the clear emphasis on word-based discourse in Scripture. His argument is that if a contemporary Christian hermeneutic is going to be adequate not only to the biblical witness, but also elucidative of our common experience of life's margins and life's wonders, then such a hermeneutic must retrieve those modes of wisdom discourse that appear *prima facie* on the boundaries of Israel's and the church's encounters with God's words and deeds on the planes of history. While Ricoeur's proposal for a rapprochement between proclamation and manifestation does weight the emphasis in favor of the Word, he maintains that the mystery of the sacred is not to be annihilated by the Word, but rather taken up into the Word's reemployment of cosmic symbolism as a support for the new history and new language revealed by God to the community. "Everything indicates therefore that the cosmic symbolism does not die, but is instead transformed in passing from the realm of the sacred to that of proclamation. The new Zion prophetically inverts the reminiscence of the sacred city, just as the Messiah who is to come projects into the eschatological future the glorious royal figures of divine unction. And for Christians, Golgotha becomes a new *axis mundi*. Every new language is also the reemployment of an ancient symbolism."[33] In this way, the ancient symbols can speak again by providing the needed resonances to our primordial experiences of a sacred cosmos. And in this provision, these symbols expand, deepen, and energize the Word's potential for procla-

---

[32]Gerhard von Rad's theology of the Old Testament is representative of the traditional position that while wisdom literature is not unessential to Israel's faith, it is on the circumference of it both theologically and textually. (Gerhard von Rad, *Old Testament Theology*, trans. D. M. G.Stalker, 2 vols. [New York: Harper & Row, 1962] 1:435-36).

[33]Ricoeur, "Manifestation and Proclamation," 33.

mation to all of us who experience the world as a ready manifestation of benevolent Mystery.

• The Promise of Theological-Literary Interpretation •

The varieties of biblical discourse has been Ricoeur's controlling interest since his earliest work in biblical studies. In the 1960s he reflected on the symbol-rich environment of the Book of Genesis; in the 1970s he considered the extravagant parables of Jesus in the Gospels; and today his theological hermeneutic is concerned with narrative discourse in both Testaments, the biblical genre we have yet to consider in this analysis. While each of these projects is related, one wonders whether his developing hermeneutic will ever fulfill its rich promise because, for a variety of reasons, much of Ricoeur's recent writing in this area remains unpublished, including a book-length manuscript entitled "Time and Narrative in the Bible: Toward a Narrative Theology," and another article with a similar title.[34] Yet a glimpse into this larger project is provided by his 1985 study of the Gospel of Mark, "Le récit interprétatif. Exégèse et Théologie dans les récits de la Passion."[35] It is to this essay, then, that I turn my final attention in order to ask whether Ricoeur's combination of theological reflection and literary theory in his exegesis of Mark suggests important new directions for hermeneutics today.

Ricoeur's advance beyond some models in theological hermeneutics is apparent in his twofold recognition of the place of the reader and the role of mixed genres in the understanding of the Bible's literary-theological world. Much of the current work in theological hermeneutics is a variation on different narrative theologies, and, like these theologies, it often suffers from an inability to account for the unnerving polysemy and the factor of the audience in determining the meaning of its main documentary source, the Bible. By comparing Ricoeur's hermeneutical theory with his exegetical practice in interpreting Mark, we will see one way that the reflective reader can uncover what I take to be (by way of Ricoeur) Jesus' Markan identity—an identity that is a function of a conflicted and esoteric plot-line (with an ambiguous protagonist and suspended ending) engendered by the different literary genres at work in the account.

---

[34]Paul Ricoeur, "Time and Narrative in the Bible: Toward a Narrative Theology," Sarum Lectures, Oxford University, 1980. Also referred to in this essay is idem, "Toward a Narrative Theology: Its Necessity, Its Resources, Its Difficulties," paper presented at Symposium on Narrative Theology, Haverford College, 1982. I want to acknowledge Paul Ricoeur's kind permission to refer to these unpublished manuscripts.

[35]In *Recherches de Science Religieuse* 73 (1985): 17-38. I want to acknowledge David Pellauer's permission to use his translation of this article.

Ricoeur's biblical narratology is significantly different from current mainline narrative theologies. Unlike these approaches,[36] Ricoeur's hermeneutic does not privilege (ironically) the genre of narrative as the principal medium through which the Bible communicates its message. Barth's argument that all theology *in nuce* should be a sustained retelling of the biblical sagas casts a long shadow over contemporary Christian theology and its concern with narrative. Ricoeur, however, wonders if this Barthian assumption does not have more to do with our fundamental love for coherent stories and dramas than it does with a balanced reading of the Bible in its conflicted play of multiple meanings and genres.

Ricoeur acknowledges the importance of biblical narrative in structuring the founding events of Israel's and the church's past. It is the Bible's employment of narrative discourse that insures the permanence of the historical dimension to the Jewish and Christian traditions, as the remembrance of a history in which God spoke and acted. But, as we have seen, Ricoeur seeks to do justice to the many genres at work in the formation of the Bible's world: as narrative rightly emphasizes the place of epoch-making events as the foundation of the Bible's history and institutions, prophecy accents the inaugural importance of the Word of God · in creating Israel's and the church's faith, and wisdom reminds the people of God of their prior belonging to a natural order charged with ambiguity and mystery. The recognition that Scripture is a cross-fertilization between different literary genres and their corresponding theological itineraries preserves the polyphony of biblical revelation, the phenomenon of intertextuality in which different aspects of the divine revealing are given full play.

Ricoeur seeks a balance between the play of differences and the strategies of coherence within Scripture. The Bible is a complicated intertext characterized by the interpretation of competing genres and themes—not a stable book dominated by the Jesus story, as many narrative theologians maintain. Ricoeur's critics (like Hans Frei) have long wondered, however, if his intertextualism is not a notion borrowed from poststructuralism that he imports into his exegesis rather than a determinative feature of the Bible discovered by a close reading of the texts themselves. Frei criticizes Ricoeur for using Continental theoretical notions such as "reader," "discourse," and "genre" in discussing the Bible's diversity

---

[36]Among others, see in this regard Hans Frei, *The Identity of Jesus Christ: The Hermeneutical Bases of Dogmatic Theology* (Philadelphia: Fortress Press, 1975); Gabriel Fackre, *The Christian Story*, rev. ed. (Grand Rapids MI: Eerdmans Publishing Co., 1984); and Ronald F. Thiemann, *Revelation and Theology* (Notre Dame IN: University of Notre Dame Press, 1985).

because such notions threaten to overwhelm the text's clear sense.[37] Yet Ricoeur makes clear that he uses general hermeneutical categories only insofar as they are dialectically related to, and not in control of, actual exegetical practice: hermeneutical theory *guides* our understanding of the text while the text's unique referents of ultimacy (i.e., God, Jesus, Kingdom of God, and so on) *govern* our understanding of the Bible's meaning.[38] Be this as it may, one must wonder if Ricoeur is really speaking of the Bible for the Christian community when he accents its differences rather than its thematic unity. What possible benefit to a Christian narrative theology is a hermeneutic that emphasizes the Bible's conflicts in style and genre at the expense of its clear and unified depictions of Jesus in the Gospels?

These are the hard questions that Frei and other theologians interested in narrative continue to put to Ricoeur. Despite many differences, contemporary narrative theologians generally assume some variation on the neoorthodox *Heilsgeschichte* thesis that the Bible's dominant mode of presentation is historylike or narrative discourse, and that theology should reflect this fact by primarily seeking to clarify the contemporary meaning of the great biblical stories of creation, exodus, exile, Jesus, the church, and the coming kingdom. As did Barth, Frei argues that the Bible is best construed as a sustained story unified by the character of Jesus in the Gospels, and that a literal or realistic reading of this story best renders the objective identity of Jesus by keeping the story free from the corrosive influence of the reader's subjective impressions in determining the story's meaning. In his earlier work, in fact, Frei maintains that the Bible's core material—the historylike stories in the Gospels—is "directly accessible" as long as the reader does not "encumber" the accounts with her own exegetical devices.

> The aim of an exegesis which simply looks for the sense of a story (but does not identify sense with religious significance for the reader) is in the final analysis that of reading the story itself. We ask if we agree on what we find there, and we discover its patterns to one another. And therefore the theoretical devices we use to make our reading more alert, appropriate, and intelligent ought to be designed to leave the story itself as unencumbered as possible. This is additionally true because *realistic stories . . . are directly accessible*. As I have noted, *they mean what they say* [emphases mine].[39]

---

[37]See Hans W. Frei, "The 'Literal Reading' of the Biblical Narrative in the Christian Tradition: Does It Stretch or Will It Break?" in *The Bible and the Narrative Tradition*, ed. Frank McConnell (New York: Oxford University Press, 1986) 36-77.

[38]Paul Ricoeur, "Philosophical Hermeneutics and Biblical Hermeneutics," in *Exegesis: Problems of Method and Exercises in Reading (Genesis 22 and Luke 15)*, ed. François Bovon and Gregoire Rouiller, trans. Donald G. Miller (Pittsburgh: Pickwick Press, 1978) 321-39.

[39]Frei, *Identity of Jesus Christ*, xv.

As long as the reader's own hermeneutical strategies do not significantly impact the Bible's clear message, then these texts can literally "mean what they say"—or, as Frei puts it at another point, the texts' patterns of meaning are self-evident because "there is no gap between the representation and what is represented by it."[40] Yet as Lynn Poland and other critics of Frei have noted, this proposal for an unencumbered and direct reading of the Bible excludes the inevitable contribution to the text's meaning that the active reader always makes.[41] Any text, the Bible included, is not like a storehouse filled with ordered units of meaning awaiting passive consumption; rather, it is "like an orchestration that strikes ever new resonances among its readers and that frees the text from the material of the words and brings it to a contemporary existence."[42]

If hermeneuts such as Gadamer and Ricoeur and reader-response theorists such as Hans-Robert Jauss and Wolfgang Iser are correct, then whenever a reader asks of a text basic questions of genre, syntax, style, and subject matter, she necessarily brings to the text a "horizon of expectations" about what the text can and cannot mean.[43] Far from there being no gap between what the text says and what it means, all literary classics (and especially the Gospel of Mark, as we will see) consistently revel in constructing textual gaps that dislocate the reader by opening a space between what the reader thinks the text does or should mean and what the text actually says. In the breach between the text's "voice" and the reader's "expectations," imaginary literature like the Bible employs numerous figures of speech or tropes—that is, phrases that are invested with figural meanings that are different from the phrases' standard, lexical meanings—in order to free the text from the interpretive confines placed onto it by the reader's desire for stability and closure. The only way that a text can be read for understanding (unless we are content with simply repeating its words by rote) is for the reader to ask her own period-specific questions of the text so that the gap of temporal and aesthetic distance between text and reader can be bridged (at least partially). In this way, the process of reader interrogation and textual response straddles the gap between what the text "says" by means of its formal modes of expression and what the text "means" to a particular community of in-

---

[40]Ibid., xiv.

[41]See Lynn Poland, *Literary Criticism and Biblical Hermeneutics* (Missoula MO: Scholars Press, 1985) 120-56. Also see Gary Comstock, "Truth or Meaning: Ricoeur versus Frei on Biblical Narrative," *Journal of Religion* 66 (1986): 117-40.

[42]Hans-Robert Jauss, *Toward an Aesthetic of Reception*, trans. Timothy Bahti (Minneapolis: University of Minnesota Press, 1982) 21.

[43]For the relevant bibliography, see Edgar V. McKnight, *The Bible and the Reader* (Philadelphia: Fortress Press, 1985).

terpreters in a particular time and place. While Frei has recently qualified his argument for the autonomy of the text from the reader,[44] his virtual circumscription of the Bible's range of meaning to its literal sense as a sustained realistic narrative seems to be as much a result of his own questions (his own "reader-response") concerning the story-bound character of Jesus in the Gospels as it is a fair reading of the whole biblical witness in its heterogeneous diversity.

We have observed that texts for Ricoeur are mediums of discourse where discourse is defined as someone's saying something about something to someone else.[45] The meaning of biblical discourse is produced within a dynamic triangle of relations between author ("someone saying something"), work ("about something"), and audience ("to someone else"). In this triangle the Bible emerges as a complex intertwining of narrative and non-narrative forms of expression (such as prophecy and wisdom) so that any attempt to short-circuit this variety with a predetermined focus on one particular genre and one particular character—the category of narrative and the identity of Jesus, as in Frei's case—violates the text's built-in plurality of expression. For Ricoeur, then, the role of the reader and the diverse itineraries of meaning within the Bible are inextricably linked: without a thoroughgoing recognition of the active part played by the reader in construing textual meaning, the Bible's strategies of transformation and dislocation accomplished through the play of genres are eclipsed.

If Ricoeur left the issue here, his hermeneutic would fall into the ranks of many current theological and literary deconstructive readings of the Bible in which interpretation is equivalent to exposing how scriptural discourse constructs and subverts meaning. This approach is not as concerned with the Bible's potential for theological reflection on the *topoi* of Christian faith as it is with uncovering its diffusion of meaning along an endless chain of signifiers.[46] If this were the case, Ricoeur's hermeneutic would be similar to Frank Kermode's. As a "secular critic," Kermode states that his literary interpretations of the Bible "do of course have implications for Christian belief, but such implications have no relevance to the present inquiry."[47] Ricoeur, on the other hand, is not a secular critic sin-

---

[44]See Frei, " 'Literal Reading' of the Biblical Narrative," 61-67.

[45]Ricoeur, "Biblical Hermeneutics," 66.

[46]In spite of some differences, on this point many poststructuralist readers of the Bible are in agreement. See, for example, Frank Kermode, *The Genesis of Secrecy: On the Interpretation of Narrative* (Cambridge: Harvard University Press, 1979); Charles E. Winquist, *Epiphanies of Darkness* (Philadelphia: Fortress Press, 1986); and Mark C. Taylor, *Erring: A Postmodern A/theology* (Chicago: University of Chicago Press, 1984).

[47]Kermode, *Genesis of Secrecy*, 101.

gularly concerned with the Bible's semantic puzzles and obscurities but a "listener to Christian preaching" who uses a biblical hermeneutic that departs from and returns to a prior commitment to Christian belief—a hermeneutic, as we noted, that "boldly stays within this circle" of Bible-informed faith.[48] As such, he is not content with simply exposing the fault-lines in the biblical topography, as is the case with many poststructuralist literary critics such as Kermode or theologians such as Mark C. Taylor. While aware of the conflicted surplus of meaning in the Bible, he never-theless suggests ways that the data of his polyphonic exegesis can be used as the raw material for systematic theological and christological reflec-tion. "Le récit interprétatif" does just this by attempting to articulate the theological coherence *through* the intertextual difference at work in the complicated account of Jesus' "present yet absent" identity in the Gospel of Mark.

• Parsimony of Presence in Mark •

"C'est en racontant que [Marc] interprète de Jesus."[49] This gospel is an in-terpreting narrative: rather than simply chronicling the discrete events of Jesus' life, Mark interprets them theologically by interweaving Jesus' words and actions into a purposeful pattern. He does this through the use of the key word *betrayed*: the gospel is surfeited with incidents of de-nial, betrayal, abandonment, treason, and flight. Mark's gospel com-bines story and history, kerygmatic necessity and contingent event. Contingency: details concerning the open-ended questioning of the dis-ciples at the Last Supper ("Is it I, Lord?"); Jesus' last-minute desire to have, if possible, the cup of suffering taken from him; and Pilate's indecision concerning Jesus' proper fate—all of this creates the impression of a real chronology consisting of the disparate events of Jesus' ministry. Neces-sity: the thematic refrain, "The Son of Man *must* be handed over," and the predictions of Judas's treason and Peter's abandonment set up the movement of the story toward its theologically predetermined end in which Jesus' betrayal into the hands of sinners is viewed as integral to his saving purpose.

Literary analysis shows how *Leitworten* such as *betrayed* function to link elements of episodic contingency and theological necessity in the story. The narrative performs its kerygmatic and apologetic intentions by achieving a subtle literary unity between what did happen (Jesus is be-trayed) and what had to have happened (Jesus must be handed over). Correspondingly, two visions of time are given full play in the narrative: Jesus prays that the chronological "hour" of his suffering might pass, but

---

[48]Ricoeur, "Naming God," 215.

[49]Paul Ricoeur, "Le récit interprétatif. Exégèse et Théologie dans le récits de la Passion," *Recherches de Science Religieuse* 73 (1985): 22.

he also recognizes that the messianic "hour" within God's masterplan has
arrived: "The hour has come" (Mark 14:41). "Henceforth the eschatological hour and the chronological hour coincide."[50] In the process, Jesus'
unified identity is rendered as a historical individual who *did* suffer and
was betrayed, and as the Son of Man who *had* to suffer and be betrayed.
Ricoeur argues that historical critics have often noted in Mark the patch-
work of different christologies based on different life-situations in the early
church. Where these critics have failed, however, is in not moving beyond this recognition to scrutinize the literary and theological coherence
at work in the equation between the historical Jesus and the predetermined Son of Man in the final redaction of Mark's gospel. "If such is the
case, to explicate this gospel means looking for the indications of the
equation it posits between its christology of a suffering Son of Man and
the story of the betrayed Jesus. The chain that these indications constitute makes the passion narrative into a literary unity, whatever may be
the history of its tradition or of its redaction."[51]

In his gospel, Mark struggles to preserve the memory and pathos of
Jesus' actual suffering. Consequently, he subverts the hellenistic theology of the victorious divine man through graphic portrayals of Jesus' concrete suffering and ignominious death. Even the title Son of God, which
could return the story to a theology of glory, is "emptied of its divine man
signification by the important addition that the centurion 'saw that he thus
breathed his last.' "[52] Mark's theology of the suffering Son of Man gen-
erates the christological irony in the crucifixion scene, for now it is the
centurion, not the fleeing disciples, who correctly interprets Jesus' identity as the Son of God in light of his humiliating and powerless death on
the cross. Mark works hard to convince the reader that Jesus' life and death
is not a christology of glory. Only a theology of the suffering Son of Man
can help the reader identify with the lived experience of the Master's suffering and provide a meaningful precedent for the persecution attendant
upon discipleship. Jesus does not simply undergo a painful death in Mark;
rather, the Markan Jesus is the Son of Man who suffers and whose suffering, as both contingent fact and theological necessity, becomes God's
atoning event for the redemption of humankind.

The theological upshot of Mark's concentration on a christology of
suffering versus a christology of glory is a certain limitation on Jesus'
presence in the gospel. Obscurity and secrecy characterize this version of
the gospel story. Ricoeur borrows Kermode's notion of the "unfollow-
able world" in the Gospels: "We know by now that we must not look in

---

[50]Ibid., 33.

[51]Ibid., 20.

[52]Ibid., 29.

Mark for those regular accumulations of narrative sense which we habitually regard as the marks of a well-formed narrative. Instead we are jostled from one puzzle to the next—immediately, again, *euthus, palin*—as if the purpose of the story were less to establish a comfortable sequence than to pile one crux on another, each instituting an intense thematic opposition."[53] Mark offers us a broken narrative with no clear story line and no transparent development of character. In Mark, Jesus reveals his mission in occult parables that outsiders are not allowed to understand; he commands those whom he has healed not to reveal his true identity; and most remarkable of all, assuming 16:8 to be the original ending, Mark abruptly terminates his gospel with the fear and silence of the women who find not Jesus, but an unidentified young man at the mouth of the tomb who announces "He has risen, he is not here." At the very point where the other gospels champion the triumphant resurrection of Jesus Christ as the fitting end to their narratives, Mark tersely identifies Jesus as the "risen absent" who is now not present but who will come again to the disciples in the future. This "parsimony of presence" in Mark's version of Jesus' postmortem existence fits well with the Christology of suffering interwoven throughout the narrative: Jesus in death is as obscure and enigmatic as he was in life. Ricoeur surmises, then, that 16:8 is the appropriate conclusion to the gospel—if not for historical-critical reasons, then certainly for literary-theological reasons—because it preserves the mystery of Jesus' mission and identity.

> It is in relation to this narrative structure with a kerygmatic function that we may attempt to interpret one unique feature of Mark's narrative, namely that the only ones present at the tomb are the women, no guards (as in Matthew), no disciples (as in Luke and John), and not even the figure of Jesus himself (as in Matthew and John). This parsimony of presence . . . continues to oppose a christology that would immediately lead to a christology of glory, short-circuiting the Master's suffering and the difficulty of being a disciple.[54]

Far from setting forth a clumsy ending that abruptly terminates Jesus' mission in the form of the women's silence and fear, the gospel, according to Ricoeur, is a subtle apology for a Christology of the suffering Son of Man that does not give short shrift to the *via dolorosa* of the historical Jesus. Ricoeur disagrees with historical-critical readings of Mark that regard Mark's compilation of his sources as primitive, wooden, and awkwardly disjointed. Beginning with Strauss's *Life of Jesus* and continuing through the better part of this century, much of the establishment his-

---

[53]Kermode, *Genesis of Secrecy*, 141.

[54]Ricoeur, "récit interprétatif," 37.

torical criticism of Mark has concluded that "the Markan account is inherently unintelligible."[55]

Ricoeur acknowledges this long-standing criticism and points out that Mark is a series of fractured surfaces, literary fault-lines, overdetermined senses, and theological puzzles. Mark is not a seamless web of meaning. He maintains, however, that the gospel's disconnectedness serves as a provocation to the reader to confront perpetually the text's indeterminacy and thereby actively risk an interpretation of its possible message for a particular community of believers. Yes, the reader finds numerous loose ends here, but the text, even though it resists the demands for closure foisted on it by the reader, is not a random cacophony. Mark's discontinuity is moderated by the author's repeated use of the *kai euthus* ("and immediately") construction. Jesus' sudden and disorienting appearances, the disciples' and the crowd's amazement at his mighty works—all these motifs are held together with a sense of immediacy and alarm by the *kai euthus* phrase. Undergirded by these conjunctures of suddenness, the Gospel of Mark alternates between disclosure and concealment, mystery and openness, clarity and obscurity. On either side of the narrative, Mark is enframed by the full-formed irruption of the Son of Man in 1:15 who openly proclaims, "The time is fulfilled, the Kingdom of God is at hand, repent and believe in the Gospel," and closes as suddenly (and, some might say, as awkwardly) as it began with the opaque "risen absent" figure of Jesus laconically alluded to at the end.

Ricoeur, then, asks us whether Mark's often obscure story, a story that mixes dimensions of concordance and discordance, might be truer to life than the smoother narrative textures of Matthew, Luke, and John. Could not Mark's christological amalgam of raw power (Jesus' amazing miracles) and deathlike calm (the mo[u]rning stillness of the empty tomb and the mute women) be an expression of the author's thoughtful and nuanced literary and theological sensibilities, an intuition for what life is all about in its many dimensions, and not a sign of "inherent unintelligibility"?

Ricoeur's emphasis on Mark's concordant-discordant portrait of Jesus' ministry indicates his refusal to level off the gospel's varied modes of discourse into a straightforward narrative Christology. There is more than narrative at work in Mark. As an interpreting narrative, Mark is a gloss on earlier testimonies or prophecies concerning the Messiah; in the form of Q or a possible notebook of Old Testament prophetic texts,[56] Mark wove these christological foreshadowings into the contingent circumstances of the Jesus story. He invested with theological necessity the early episodic accounts of Jesus' life and ministry. The earlier testimonies concerning the

---

[55] Albert Schweitzer, *The Quest of the Historical Jesus*, trans. W. Montgomery (New York: Macmillan Publishing Company, 1968) 360.

[56] Kermode raises this latter possibility in *Genesis of Secrecy*, 82.

Messiah's precursor, healings, number of disciples, Second Coming, betrayal, and particulars of his death performed a double function in Mark's story: they provided the minimal events for his full-blown narrative, and they invested his narrative with prophetic authority because Mark demonstrated that they had now been fulfilled in Jesus' life and ministry.

In addition to prophecy, Mark also displays the imprint of wisdom discourse. His final portrayal of Jesus is as the risen (elsewhere) and absent (here) Son of Man whose power is in powerlessness and whose message is intentionally obscured by the messenger himself. Does not the indeterminate and open-ended character of Mark bear traces of wisdom? Are not the built-in obscurities and discrepancies in Mark echoes of the marginal wisdom literature in the Hebrew Scripture, a literature that struggles to remind us of our fragilities and insecurities while it places us in fundamental relation to the heights and depths of life itself? Here and elsewhere Ricoeur avers that wisdom discourse speaks subtly and compassionately to those contradictions within the human condition that life before a supposedly gracious God makes more acute, not less.[57] The deity of Mark is a God of the gaps: a now-here, now-invisible "presence" who exists for the community in the cracks and discontinuities of their everyday worlds. Mark's narrative, if we can call this "narrative," artfully blends the tick-tock rhythm of a story with the breakdown of narrative sense characteristic of prophetic and wisdom discourse—those disturbing genres of otherness and interruption that give the gospel its uneasy sense of disorder and lack of closure. If this is the case, Mark's gospel is a minority report in the Christian salvation scheme, one that fulfills a need that Old Testament wisdom discourse fulfilled for the people of Israel: to remind the systematic theologies of the status quo that life is riddled with complexity, that happiness is always elusive, that God, in short, is Mystery.

Contrary to some interpretations within traditional historical criticism, Mark's gospel is not a random record of disparate occurrences but rather a well-crafted literary and theological interpretation of the Christ-event that includes echoes and transformations of Old Testament prophetic discourse and the enigmatic wisdom sayings of the sages and seers. Of course, Mark is not unique among the biblical texts in weaving together previous literary styles into an integrated whole. The interplay and

---

[57]For a broader theoretical discussion of the place of wisdom and prophetic discourse in Ricoeur's hermeneutic, see Ricoeur, "Hermeneutic of Revelation," 73-118, and David Pellauer, "Paul Ricoeur on the Specificity of Religious Language," *Journal of Religion* 61 (1981): 264-84. For Ricoeur's practical application of his notion of wisdom discourse to the theodicy problem in the Hebrew Bible, see his "Evil, A Challenge to Philosophy and Theology," *Journal of the American Academy of Religion* 53 (1985): 635-50.

reconditioning of these different modes of discourse in Mark is characteristic of the whole Bible as a "living intertext"[58] that works to transform and refashion its many genres into the literary means by which various features of the divine life are made known to different communities of interpretation. By showing how the Bible's competing theological itineraries are accomplished through the interworking of these modes of discourse, Ricoeur, in my opinion, successfully mines much of Scripture's rich hermeneutical potential.

• Conclusion •

Ricoeur's narrativist reading of Mark is not unique insofar as numerous exegetes are now employing literary analysis in the study of the Gospels,[59] even as his call for linking the tasks of narrative theory and Christian theology is a call many theologians and literary theorists have sounded today as well. His importance lies in his insistence that a narratological approach to the Bible must include a complete sensitivity to the role of the audience and the variety of discourses at work in the formation of the Bible's literary and theological world. At present, many deconstructionist scholars of the Bible and Christian thought truncate the hermeneutical task by refusing to risk an interpretation of the unifying theological themes in the Bible. On the other side, many narrative theologians offer a homophonic reading of the Jesus story with little awareness of how that story is interpenetrated and overdetermined by the other modes of biblical discourse that are non-narrative. By the same token, we have seen how Mark's consistent christological themes are articulated to the active reader through the crisscrossing of genres so that (with important qualifications) both the poststructuralist concern for difference and the narrative theologians' interest in coherence is preserved. Ricoeur's hermeneutic—as a via media between mainline narrative theology and secular literary readings of the Bible—provides the framework for a Christian theology that emerges from the *fête du sens*[60] within Hebrew Scripture and the New Testament, the play of interdependent voices that projects a world of unimagined possibilities for the believer-reader.

---

[58]Ricoeur, "Time and Narrative in the Bible," 1:6.

[59]For three representative examples in Markan studies, see Werner H. Kelber, *The Kingdom in Mark* (Philadelphia: Fortress Press, 1974); David Rhoads and Donald Michie, *Mark as Story* (Philadelphia: Fortress Press, 1982); and J. Lee Magness, *Sense and Absence* (Atlanta: Scholars Press, 1986).

[60]Ricoeur, "théologie de la parole," 314.

THE SECOND NAIVETÉ
IN BARTH AND RICOEUR

When the distinctions have been made they can be pushed again into the background and the whole can be read (with this tested and critical naiveté) as the totality it professes to be.[1]

Does that mean that we could go back to a primitive naiveté? Not at all. In every way, something has been lost, irremediably lost: immediacy of belief. But if we can no longer live the great symbolisms of the sacred in accordance with the original belief in them, we can, we modern men, aim at a second naiveté in and through criticism. In short, it is by interpreting *that we can hear* again.[2]

• Following the Hermeneutical Arc •

After considering separately Barth's and Ricoeur's thought, it is now time to take up the points of similarity and difference in the hermeneutical programs of each. What I find compellingly common in both thinkers is their willingness to risk strong readings of the Bible by taking seriously its claim to confront the reader with the Word of God. This willingness is at odds both with many traditional historical-critical interpreters who limit the Bible's range of reference to its historical and authorial background and at odds with contemporary postmodern critics who cut the nerve cord between the Bible's internal literary environment and the extralinguistic world of meaning outside the text. In both cases the Bible's power to unfold a world that the reader could risk inhabiting—a world beyond the Bible's background, on the one hand, and literary conventions, on the other—is unfortunately lost.

---

[1]Karl Barth, *Church Dogmatics*, vol. 4:2, trans. G. W. Bromiley (Edinburgh: T. and T. Clark, 1958) 479.

[2]Paul Ricoeur, *The Symbolism of Evil*, trans. Emerson Buchanan (Boston: Beacon Press, 1967) 351.

Barth's and Ricoeur's argument that Scripture should be allowed to mean all that it possibly can mean is methodologically clarified in their related proposals that theological hermeneutics follow a three-step method for interpreting the Word in the words of the biblical witness. Interpretation follows an arc that consists of an initial pregrasp of the text's subject matter as a whole (understanding); a later construal of the text's constituent parts that make up the whole (explanation); and last, a final understanding of the relation between the text's parts and the whole, an understanding that engenders a fusion between the world of the text and the world of the reader (appropriation). In this section I hope to show how this common method in both Barth and Ricoeur can open up to the reader a mature innocence, a second naiveté, toward the vision of reality projected by the biblical witness.

Barth's major discussion of the process of hermeneutics is found in *Church Dogmatics* 1:2, "Freedom under the Word," pages 722-40. His handling of a wide variety of biblical texts and church doctrines receives its guidelines from the carefully developed three-step method outlined in this section of 1:2. Barth, however, was primarily interested in the *practice* of interpreting Scripture and was always wary of discussions concerning which hermeneutical *method* (be it his or another's) should be used to undergird such practice. Yet his caveat against the dangers of method-specific interpretation should not obscure the important role his own exegetical model does in fact play in his theological reflection, even though some of Barth's interpreters do not recognize the place of this model in his overall theology.[3]

Barth delineates three moments or phases in what he labels "the one totality of scriptural interpretation"[4]: Observation (*Beobachtung, explicatio, sensus*); Reflection (*Nachdenken, meditatio*); and Appropriation (*Aneignung, applicatio, usus*). Each of these moments constitutes a single process of in-

---

[3]Many of Barth's interpreters have often overlooked the significance of his work on hermeneutics in 1:2 for his overall theological project. David Ford, for example, argues that with regard to Barth's exegetical method "1:1 and 2, seem to me to be surprisingly inessential to understanding the later volumes" (Ford, *Barth and God's Story: Biblical Narrative and the Theological Method of Karl Barth in the "Church Dogmatics"* [Frankfurt am Main and Bern: Peter Lang, 1981] 24). But as in the case of any systematic thinker, it seems hermeneutically suspect to read later sections of that thinker's work in relative isolation from what preceded them. It is noteworthy that Barth outlined with care his hermeneutical method in the prefatory volume of his dogmatics. The introduction of this topic in the prolegomena to the *Dogmatics* functions analogously to his inception of the doctrine of the Trinity in 1:1: the inauguration of each topic at its respective juncture sets the theological stage for what later follows, even though neither topic as such is discussed again on a sustained basis.

[4]Barth, *Church Dogmatics* 1:2, 736.

vestigating the meaning of the biblical texts to the end that the exegete's life and thinking become conformed to the scriptural message. The three moments are separate but related, as each phase mutually depends on and extends the insights generated from the preceding phase or phases. Although previous exegetes and theologians have used a similar tripartite program,[5] Barth's appropriation of this method is original because he uses it as a heuristic for explicating the world of the Bible as a world to which the interpreter can comport herself anew.

The first observation phase is the "unravelling or unfolding of the scriptural word" in order to form a "picture" or "image" of the text's subject matter.[6] The process of picture formation follows the reference of the text's message: "My aim is to convey the subject-matter or reference of what the author says in this particular text. In this way I obtain a picture of his expression, and I then compare this with other things which the same author has said about the same thing and with what he has said on other matters."[7] In forming a "picture" of a world that is decisively more important (and more real, so to speak) than the common world we inhabit, we unravel a self-contained totality that "must have unconditional precedence over all the evidence of our own being and becoming, our own thoughts and endeavors, hope and suffering, of all the evidence of intellect and senses, of axioms and theorems, which we inherit and as such bear with us."[8] Here is a world charged with imaginative variations on reality. In this world the reader finds a new openness to the possibility of her presuppositions about the text—and reality in general—being thoroughly displaced and then replaced by the text's subject matter.

The guiding idea that informs the moment of observation is "fidelity in all circumstances to the object reflected in the words of the prophets and apostles."[9] Without a tenacious adherence to the biblical object, interpretation falters on our preconceived ideas as to who God is and how God relates to the world. It is here that Barth's celebrated problem with Rudolf Bultmann comes to the fore, where he maintains that his Marburg colleague has so focused on the problems of the New Testament's troublesome mythological language that the incumbent hermeneutical task of

---

[5] Barth mentions Polanus as an example (*Church Dogmatics* 1:2, 721-22), and, as we will see below, Ricoeur's three-step hermeneutical method is very similar to Barth's model.

[6] Barth, *Church Dogmatics* 1:2, 722-24.

[7] Ibid., 723.

[8] Ibid., 719.

[9] Ibid., 725.

uncovering Scripture's subject matter has been overshadowed.[10] This latter task is both the more proper and more difficult one; it is the task of observation, where we first grapple with the text's message and then deal with the question of how this message is to be presented to the modern world. Bultmann, by contrast, contends that unless the message is first translated into terms accessible to modern people, the process of understanding the truth of the kerygma is impossible. "If the truth of the New Testament proclamation is to be preserved, the only way is to demythologize it."[11]

But this is not the task of observation, according to Barth: "Our first endeavor must be to stop and listen to what the New Testament actually says. Then, indeed, as we seek to grasp the message of the New Testament, we must grapple with the task of translation and somewhere confront contemporary man. The task of translation is a secondary concern, and it can only be done well if both reader and exegete take in hand the primary task first."[12] We cannot translate before we have interpreted, and we cannot interpret until we have settled the issue of what the text in question is fundamentally about. Barth argues that Bultmann has neglected this first priority of struggling with the text's subject matter in deference to what Barth deems the secondary task of translating the New Testament into contemporary idiom.

Bultmann's consistent rejoinder to Barth was that the gospel's demand for our authentic decision is not yielded unless the New Testament is first responsibly demythologized. Bultmann's intent was to present the biblical kerygma in its full existential address to the human person—albeit an address now cut free from its historical and literary moorings. But it is precisely these moorings (according to Barth) that anchor the message in time and history and give the message a concrete relevance and full-bodiedness that it does not have when it is reduced to a set of image-poor propositions abstracted from the rich stories and language of Scripture. Barth asks rhetorically "whether it is right to stigmatize everything mythological as though it were *ipso facto* absolutely useless for modern man. Why should not the divine be described in terms of human life, the

---

[10]Karl Barth, "Rudolf Bultmann—An Attempt to Understand Him," in *Kerygma and Myth*, ed. Hans-Werner Bartsch, 2 vols. (London: S.P.C.K., 1962) 2:83-132.

[11]Rudolf Bultmann, "New Testament and Mythology," in *Kerygma and Myth*, 1:10. Bultmann's point is that because the "kerygma is incredible to modern man, for he is convinced that the mythical view of the world is obsolete . . . theology must undertake the task of stripping the kerygma from its mythological framework, of 'demythologizing' it" (ibid., 3).

[12]Barth, "Rudolf Bultmann," 88.

otherworldly in terms of this world, the nonobjective as objective?"[13] By attempting to separate the Bible's *content* from its *form*, Bultmann has purchased a kind of barren relevance for the kerygma at the price of preserving the central message of Scripture—a message that is incommensurably given in the multitextured stories about Jesus Christ in all their historical, symbolic, and mythological fullness.

Barth's point is that because Bultmann begins in the wrong place—emphasizing the translatability of the gospel before first seeking fidelity to the gospel itself—he has lost what he sought to preserve: a faithful retelling of the biblical witness so the reader might have a new future in conformity with the biblical world view. Barth maintains that the retelling of the biblical message in proclamation cannot, and need not, be separated from its original telling in Scripture for the sake of theology's conversation with the world. When the gospel form is bracketed away from its content, the inevitable result is that the message itself suffers either a "narrowing down"[14] to an ahistorical abstraction, or it is lost entirely due to our focus on the problematic context—however disconcerting to modern sensibilities—that surrounds the message. Barth can defend, with Bultmann, the need for some type of disciplined demythologization, but nothing is gained by the introduction of "some criterion to enable us to know in advance what parts of the text are intelligible, and thus differentiate the *outward imagery* from the *actual substance*" [emphasis mine].[15] Preserving the union between a text's imagery and substance, its form and content, is required of any theological hermeneutic that seeks to present the whole Word of God in its totality as revealed, proclaimed, *and* written.

Ricoeur's hermeneutic, formally speaking, follows the same three-step method that Barth uses in order to understand better the biblical witness to the Word of God. Ricoeur and his interpreters have formulated the three stages of interpretation in different ways, and I find that each of these related formulations has enriched the understanding of Ricoeur's triadic method.[16] In response to Lewis Mudge's collection of Ricoeur's essays on

---

[13]Ibid., 108.

[14]Ibid., 95.

[15]Ibid., 108.

[16]David Klemm refers to Ricoeur's three stages of interpretation as "first naiveté," "critique," "second naiveté" (Klemm, *The Hermeneutical Theory of Paul Ricoeur* [Lewisburg PA: Bucknell Press, 1983] 69); Lewis Mudge uses the terms "testimony in the making," "critical moment," "post-critical moment" (Mudge, "Paul Ricoeur on Biblical Interpretation," in *Essays on Biblical Interpretation*, ed. Lewis S. Mudge [Philadelphia: Fortress Press, 1980] 18-32); David Tracy prefers the simple formulation "understanding," "explanation," "understanding" (Tracy, *The Analogical Imagination: Christian Theology and the Culture of Pluralism* [New York:

biblical interpretation, Ricoeur summarized his previous position and offers these three moments in the process of biblical hermeneutics: naive understanding, objective explanation, and appropriation.[17] Or, as he puts it more recently in his work on the unity of time and narrative in a theory of threefold mimesis, all understanding follows an arc that begins with an initial preunderstanding of reality that we bring *to* the text (mimesis 1), the restructuring and configuration of this initial understanding of reality *by* the text (mimesis 2), and the final intersection *between* the world configured by the text and the world of the reader (mimesis 3).[18]

The first stage is to allow the text to say all that it possibly can say by risking an initial understanding or "guess" as to what the text means. This entails, as we noted in chapter 2, recognizing the text as a work of discourse separated from the mental intentions of its author and the historical circumstances within which the text was written. As such, the text has a plenitude of possible meanings on the basis of its subscription to the different forms of literary production (i.e., composition, genre, and style) that make the text a publicly accessible work. If our initial understanding of the text cannot be secured by an appeal to authorial intention, then the interpreter must estimate, even "guess," what the text might mean in light of its semantic structure as a literary work. "The problem of the correct understanding can no longer be solved by a simple return to the alleged situation of the author. The concept of guess has no other origin. To construe the meaning as the verbal meaning of the text is to make a guess."[19]

As problematic as the term *guess* is to explicate this first stage, Ricoeur uses this word to underscore the fundamental historicality of human knowing in the process of textual interpretation. With Barth and Gadamer, we have seen that all reflection is mediated and that our understanding of texts is necessarily perspectival and presuppositional; textual understanding involves my "standing here" with a pregrasp of the meaning of the text in general as the necessary precondition for comprehending the composite nature of the text's "standing there." The inter-

---

Crossroad Press, 1981] 151-52, n. 107); and Gibson Winter adapts Ricoeur's model for the interpretation of both literary and societal "texts" under the rubrics "guessing or discerning," "explanation," "comprehension" (Gibson Winter, *Liberating Creation: Foundations of Religious Social Ethics* [New York: Crossroad Press, 1981] 80-89).

[17]Paul Ricoeur, "Reply to Lewis S. Mudge," in *Essays on Biblical Interpretation*, 43-44.

[18]Paul Ricoeur, *Time and Narrative*, trans. Kathleen McLaughlin and David Pellaeur, 3 vols. (Chicago: University of Chicago Press, 1984–1988) 1:52-87.

[19]Paul Ricoeur, *Interpretation Theory: Discourse and the Surplus of Meaning* (Fort Worth: Texas Christian University Press, 1976) 76.

pretive process is circular and reciprocal because one cannot understand the text as a whole without some understanding of its individual parts; yet apart from an initial construal of the meaning of the whole, the parts as individual units of meaning make no sense.

The "guess" issues in a rough attempt to unfold the world of the biblical texts as an integrated, meaningful whole. Yet the biblical text-world, like any other literary world, is organized by the literary codes or modes of discourse that not only characterize, but also produce all written discourse as a work. Consequently, one of Ricoeur's most distinctive contributions to biblical hermeneutics has been to locate, as we saw in his exegesis of Mark, the *forms* of discourse—narratives, proverbs, laws, wisdom sayings, and so on—that have stuctured the biblical texts in order to explain the meaning of these texts' *content*. It is not enough to affirm Scripture's power to communicate; for Ricoeur, we have to explain *how* the Bible means in light of its modes of discourse. "It is not enough to say that religious language is meaningful, that it is not senseless, that it makes sense, that it has a meaning of its own, and so forth. We have to say that its meanings are ruled and guided by the modes of articulation specific to each mode of discourse."[20] At work in Ricoeur's concern for the biblical modes of discourse is a principle borrowed from general hermeneutics that has tremendous import for biblical interpretation: the text's literary form cannot be separated from its content without an irreparable loss of meaning. In hermeneutics, then, it follows that there is an "affinity between a form of discourse and a certain modality of the confession of faith"[21] that has critical theological significance in interpretation. We begin with a specification of the forms of discourse characteristic of the text in question so that in a first, naive understanding of the text's literary forms, its theological contents will be rendered transparent.

It is instructive to note that Ricoeur, as did Barth, faults Bultmann's existential hermeneutic of the New Testament on precisely this issue. Ricoeur is well known, and rightly so, for his argument that a theological hermeneutic completes its task only in the moment of personal appropriation when the claims of the text are applied to the concrete experience of the interpreter. "The text accomplishes its meaning only in personal appropriation."[22] But the movement from the text's *meaning* to its life *significance* for the interpreter is an arduous task, fraught with difficulties that should not be short-circuited by premature attention to the text's demand for personal obedience. The transfer from text to life, from mean-

[20]Paul Ricoeur, "Philosophy and Religious Language," *Journal of Religion* 54 (1974): 75.

[21]Ibid., 74. Also see Ricoeur, "Toward a Hermeneutic of the Idea of Revelation," in *Essays on Biblical Interpretation*, 90-92.

[22]Paul Ricoeur, "Preface to Bultmann," in *Essays on Biblical Interpretation*, 68.

ing to significance must be made, but the path between each pole should be traveled with patience lest the subject matter of the biblical world be forgotten in our quest for its existential meaning. The initial task of hermeneutics is simply to facilitate the display of this world, not stimulate a decision for or against this world on the part of the reader, "but to allow the unfolding of the world of being which is the 'thing' of the biblical text."[23] Bultmann's guiding hermeneutic, on the other hand, is that the question of authentic human existence as obedience to the kerygma is the issue of the New Testament. In Ricoeur's view, Bultmann short-circuits the long and tenuous connection between textual meaning and existential decision by "interpreting the cosmological and mythological statements of the Bible in terms of human existence."[24]

Bultmann's exegesis jeopardizes the display of the text in its fullness because it seeks (via demythologization) to uncover the text's existential *content* apart from its literary *form*, to divorce the raw demands of the biblical kerygma from the kerygma's mythological accretions. For Ricoeur and Barth, however, the biblical texts' kerygmatic message is inextricably bound up with the Bible's modes of literary expression, so that any attempt to separate the former from the latter results in a loss of the text's full meaning. Though Ricoeur agrees with Bultmann's stress on the text's internal demand for existential appropriation, he contends that this emphasis comes too early in Bultmann's hermeneutics. Before the text's demands on the reader can be met, biblical hermeneutics must uncover and display the text's objective and ideal meaning as that meaning has continued through time; the semantic moment must precede the existential moment at the early stage of interpretation so that the text can speak in its ideality before it is appropriated by the reader.

> The moment of exegesis is not that of existential decision but that of "meaning," which, as Frege and Husserl have said, is an objective and even an "ideal" moment (ideal in that meaning has no place in reality, not even in psychic reality). Two thresholds of understanding then must be distinguished, the threshold of "meaning," which is what I just described, and that of "signification," which is the moment when the reader grasps the meaning, the moment when the meaning is actualized in existence. The

---

[23]Paul Ricoeur, "Philosophical Hermeneutics and Biblical Hermeneutics," in *Exegesis: Problems of Method and Exercises in Reading (Genesis 22 and Luke 15)*, ed. François Bovon and Gregoire Rouiller, trans. Donald G. Miller (Pittsburgh: Pickwick Press, 1978) 330.

[24]Ricoeur's lucid exposition of Bultmann's hermeneutics can be found in his "Preface to Bultmann," 49-72. The quotation is from p. 70 of this article. For a clear discussion of the hermeneutical differences between Ricoeur and Bultmann, see Lynn Poland, *Literary Criticism and Biblical Hermeneutics* (Missoula MO: Scholars Press, 1985) chap. 4.

entire route of comprehension goes from the ideality of meaning to existential signification. A theory of interpretation which at the outset runs
straight to the moment of decision moves too fast.[25]

The first task is to allow the text to display its world (be it mythological
or nonmythological, cosmic or individual, primordial or modern) and then
raise the issue concerning this world's contemporary and existential import. We first ask what the text says as an object of meaning and then
question what it means for the interpreting subject.

This point underscores Barth's and Ricoeur's mutual disagreement
with Bultmann's hermeneutic. The fundamental problem with a com-
bined demythologization-existential hermeneutic is that it grants priority
to our modern presupposition that God can only be understood by us in
a decontextualized language of decision unemcumbered by the mythological framework that carries the biblical message. As Ricoeur argues,
however, "It is necessary for us to struggle also with the presuppositions
of modern man himself, with the presupposition of his modernity."[26] This
is Barth's criticism of Bultmann as well: our enlightened presuppositions
that determine at the outset what the text can and cannot mean only con-
firm our self-understandings and undermine the possibility of a novel
encounter with the Other in the text.

Bultmann hoped to separate the Bible's nonmythological notions such
as "act of God," "word of God," and so forth from the Bible's dated,
mythological language in order to liberate the biblical kerygma as a meaningful message for contemporary interpreters. This allows the kerygma's
true scandal, its call for obediential faith, to be separated from the message's false scandal, the mythological wrappings that inhibit the kerygma's true expression. Barth and Ricoeur maintain, however, that this
separation jeopardizes the display of all the elements (mythological and
nonmythological) of the biblical world in their disorienting entirety. Insofar as these elements are inseparable from the text's meaning as a work,
these elements must be preserved in interpreting the text's significance
for the present. In broad strokes, we can say that the totality of biblical
references to a new world of being has ontological, not simply existential,
implications. The point of the biblical message is not to press the reader
for an existential decision, but to display a full world in which the interpreter is confronted with the possibility of seeing the world as the biblical
modes of discourse describe it—and therein the reader discovers that her
presuppositions about what can and cannot count as reality are ready to
be overturned. For Barth and Ricoeur, there is no direct appropriation of

---

[25]Ricoeur, "Preface to Bultmann," 68.

[26]Ricoeur, "The Language of Faith," in *The Philosophy of Paul Ricoeur: An Anthology of His Work*, ed. Charles E. Reagan and David Stewart (Boston: Beacon Press,
1978) 227.

the Word of God in the moment of existential encounter apart from the literary forms that express this Word—there is no "revelation in itself," as Barth puts it.[27]

The display of the text-world in its fullness is the first stage of interpretation—the moment of "observation" in Barth and "understanding" in Ricoeur. With Bultmann in mind, Barth and Ricoeur warn against any premature movement to the text's existential import before an adequate (albeit initial) understanding of the text's literary and theological world is deployed. This first expression of the text's world as an intertextual whole is then tested for adequacy and coherence through various explanatory devices (and their attending philosophical presuppositions). The interpreter's first grasp of the meaning of the text as a whole is not methodologically innocent, as Ricoeur says; hence, the use of explanatory resources in hermeneutics (for example, historical criticism, structural analysis, redaction criticism, and so forth) is both inevitable and necessary for understanding the text's parts in relation to the text's whole. The hermeneutical circle, then, is a productive circle that consists of our first pregrasp of the text's subject matter (understanding) and our later critical construal of the text's constituent elements (explanation) which, in turn, sets up our pregrasp as a candidate for revision in order to enable a new understanding of the text's subject matter (appropriation). It is to this middle step that I now turn my attention.

Reflection in Barth is the transition moment between *sensus* and *usus*, *explicatio* and *applicatio*. The broad picture of the text-world developed in observation is now reflected upon through a particular thought-scheme or schemes to be acted upon in the final moment of appropriation. In reflection, the exegete cannot free herself of her intellectual shadow because a world view or philosophical slant necessarily accompanies all interpretation of the biblical texts.[28] This should not be surprising, however; for as we saw in chapter 1, Barth uses the resources within both historical criticism and typological exegesis to facilitate the display of the biblical text-world. The moment of reflection highlights the necessity for this disciplined employment of different interpretive strategies to aid the hermeneutical task.

Barth holds that even the "simplest Bible reader" implicitly possesses "some sort of philosophy" that shapes the reader's reflection on the biblical texts.[29] He continues: "Even in what [the interpreter] says as an ob-

---

[27]Barth, *Church Dogmatics* 1:2, 492.

[28]Ibid., 727.

[29]Ibid., 728. See also here Barth's festschrift article for his brother Heinrich, a philosopher himself, entitled "Philosophie und Theologie," in *Philosophie und Christliche Existenz: Festschrift für Heinrich Barth zum 70. Geburtstag*, ed. Gerhard Huber (Basel and Stuttgart: Verlag Helbing & Lichtenhahn, 1960) 93-106.

server and exponent, he will everywhere betray the fact that, consciously or unconsciously, in cultured or primitive fashion, consistently or inconsistently, he has approached the text from the standpoint of a particular epistemology, logic or ethics, of definite ideas and ideals concerning the relations of God, the world and man, and that in reading and expounding the text he cannot deny these."[30] Barth maintains that all theologians have been indebted to one particular standpoint or another. The medieval scholastics, Thomas, and the orthodox Protestants appropriated Aristotle; Luther and Calvin were neo-Platonist and classical Platonist, respectively.[31] Barth does not take issue with this precedent; in fact, he identifies himself with those theologians who have self-consciously borrowed extrabiblical tools and vocabulary for the purpose of explanation. "We must remember that we are definitely ranging ourselves with those who 'explain' the Bible, i.e., read it through the spectacles of a definite system of ideas, which has the character of a 'world-view' and will in some way make itself felt as such when we read and explain the Bible. If we hold up hands of horror at the very idea, we must not forget that without such systems of explanation, without such spectacles, we cannot read the Bible at all."[32]

Calvin said that Scripture provides the "spectacles" through which we see God[33]; Barth says that philosophy yields the "spectacles" through which we read Scripture. Barth's statement is remarkable given the uneasy relationship between theology and philosophy generally found in his writing, and it is all the more surprising given his consistent criticism of other theologians for allowing the content of the Christian witness to be controlled by what he deemed to be alien philosophical forces.[34] He criticized, for example, Schleiermacher's use of a Kantian philosophy of limits to deny certain central claims of the Christian witness,[35] and he labeled Bultmann's appropriation of Heidegger's thought an "anthropo-

---

[30]Barth, *Church Dogmatics* 1:2, 728.

[31]Ibid.

[32]Ibid.

[33]John Calvin, *Institutes of the Christian Religion*, trans. Ford Lewis Battle, ed. John T. McNeill, 2 vols. (Philadelphia: Westminster Press, 1955) 1:70.

[34]Though Barth classifies himself with those theologians who use explanatory spectacles, he was always reticent to identify which spectacles his own dogmatics employs; and he regularly criticized his interpreters who sought to clarify his theological presuppositions by suggesting this or that philosophical viewpoint as influential, if not determinative, in his thought.

[35]Karl Barth, *The Theology of Schleiermacher*, trans. Geoffrey W. Bromiley, ed. Dietrich Ritschl (Grand Rapids MI: Wm. B. Eerdmans Publishing Co., 1982) 90-102.

logical straightjacket" that he himself would never have put on in order to understand the New Testament.[36] Barth was often not a fair polemicist. His understanding of the explanatory moment—to use nontheological thought as a resource for aiding but not determining the meaning of the biblical subject matter—is virtually identical to the understanding utilized by Schleiermacher and Bultmann. And though he regarded both theologians as enmeshed in philosophical systems that compromised their theologies from the start, I do not find his argument against neo-Protestantism convincing on this issue, even if his basic model for relating theology and extrabiblical categories is sound.

Under the moment of reflection, Barth gives a series of guidelines for how an extrabiblical thought-system—or philosophy, as Barth prefers—is to be used in the service of theological hermeneutics. First, no philosophy in itself is tailor-made for the Christian subject matter, no matter what its prima facie similarities to the biblical witness; rather, a philosophy is only properly fitted to the scriptural Word when it sustains an authentic encounter with the Word and is found in the Christian community to be helpful in elucidating the nature of this encounter. (One thinks of Augustine's handling of neo-Platonism in explaining his experience of the soul's *reditus* to God as an example here.)

Second, the use of philosophy in theological hermeneutics should always have the character of an essay, a hypothesis, a thought-experiment. A nontheological perspective in the service of Christian reflection is deployed in an experimental and provisional fashion. Such a perspective is a wager, a gamble: it may or may not clarify the subject matter in question, but it is worth the risk given the hermeneutical exigency to understand better the biblical subject matter. "My mode of thought may not be of any use in and by itself, but by the grace of the Word of God why should it not be able to become useful in His service? In itself, as such, it is a hypothesis: the hypothesis upon which I must venture in obedience, because I have only the alternative either of risking some other hypothesis or of not obeying at all."[37]

Third, Barth encourages an eclectic, nonsystematic use of philosophy in the service of theology. If *no* philosophy is perfectly suited for the Christian witness (so guideline 1), then no *one* philosophy should be accorded the status of the single and universal *philosophia perennis* to be used in the service of hermeneutical reflection. A thought-scheme should always respond to the concrete and specific needs of theology for the moment and not seek a more determinative position beyond its limited, ad hoc role. "In the necessary use of some scheme of thought for reflection upon what Scripture has to say, there is no essential reason for preferring

---

[36]Barth, "Rudolf Bultmann," 114.

[37]Barth, *Church Dogmatics* 1:2, 731.

one of these schemes to another. . . . The necessity which there is is particular: in a specific situation this or that particular mode of thought can
be particularly useful in scriptural exegesis, and it can then become a
command to avail oneself of it in this particular instance."[38] In principle,
any and every philosophy is a potential dialogue partner for theology.[39]
But Barth's third guideline carries a proviso: no philosophy should be allowed to dictate to theology how the normative Christian witness is to be
definitively understood and presented. If this proviso is forgotten, philosophy loses its status as a heuristic device in the service of God's Word
and becomes another absolute alongside the Word. For Barth, philosophy continues to function as the handmaiden of theology, but the handmaiden now has numerous sisters in theology's service.

This guideline summarizes the previous three. Barth acknowledges
that even theology itself is "a kind of philosophy"[40] as a form of human
reflection; like philosophy, it too must be careful not to control the scriptural witness. "In face of its object, theology itself can only wish to be *ancilla*. That is why it cannot assign any other role to philosophy. Scripture
alone can be the *domina*."[41] As George Lindbeck has rightly noted, Barth's
theology is "intratextual" because it reflects on Christian symbols in the
language and thought-forms of the Bible and does not ground these symbols on any philosophical, extrabiblical foundations.[42] Barth envisions
theology as operating within the horizon of the biblical world, and while
it cannot ahistorically extricate itself in toto from extrabiblical ideas ("If
we open our mouths we find ourselves in the province of philosophy"[43]),
it still eschews conscious dependence on any such ideas. "I as a theologian, having my language, whatever it may be, go up with that language
to an object that meets me in the witness of Holy Scripture. In making
this witness my own, I am not free of all philosophy, but at the same time
I am not bound to a definite philosophy."[44]

---

[38]Ibid., 733.

[39]Hans Frei highlights this aspect of Barth's hermeneutics and suggests that
Barth's "*ad hoc* apologetics, in order to throw into relief particular features of [the
biblical] world," employs "any and all technical philosophical concepts and conceptual schemes" to explicate the Christian subject matter ("An Afterword: Eberhard Busch's Biography of Karl Barth," in H.-Martin Rumscheidt, ed., *Karl Barth
in Re-View: Posthumous Works Reviewed and Assessed* [Pittsburgh: Pickwick Press,
1981] 114).

[40]Barth, *Church Dogmatics* 1:2, 734.

[41]Ibid., 735.

[42]George Lindbeck, *The Nature of Doctrine* (Philadelphia: Westminster Press,
1984) 135.

[43]Karl Barth, *Credo* (New York: Charles Scribner's Sons, 1962) 184.

[44]Ibid.

Barth seeks to avoid the threat of philosophical terminology to determine the content of Christian theology. While he had utilized certain categories and expressions from Platonism to existentialism in his earlier work, his mature dogmatics sought to advance an internal dialogue between the proclamation and dogmas of the church and the witness of the scriptural Word of Jesus Christ. In mediating the relationship between theology and philosophy, Barth erects a nonaggression pact between the provinces of theology and other forms of nontheological thought so that philosophy remains in the service of explicating the normative Christian witness, but is always guarded against lest it threaten to control the witness that it serves.

What is the relationship between extrabiblical thought-schemes and the Word of God in Ricoeur's thought? At first glance, his formulation of the explanatory moment lends credence to the charges of some of his interpreters, as we saw in chapter 2, that his use of hermeneutical philosophy overwhelms his attempts to offer a faithful reading of the biblical message. Initially, he maintains that the methodology of theological hermeneutics (or what he alternately calls biblical hermeneutics) is entirely consistent with that of general hermeneutics, except that the subject matter of the former (the special reality of the Word of God) is less homogeneous with philosophical discourse than the subject matter of the latter (reality as such). This difference is important, however, because it is the understanding of this governing subject matter that calls into question any simple translation of the categories and insights of general hermeneutics into the fields of theology and exegesis. Because the biblical texts semantically function as texts like other texts, theological hermeneutics relies on extratheological tools to aid the interpretation of these texts; but because it is the absolute itself that is said to be "named" in the scriptural records, theological interpretation is cautious (even suspicious) of any general interpretive strategy that might compromise the integrity of those texts which the church prizes as vehicles for the Word of God. At the midpoint of the arc we are examining here, Ricoeur is programmatically self-conscious about the precise relationship that should obtain between general and theological hermeneutics. On the one hand, theological hermeneutics is a regional species of general hermeneutics that applies general rules of interpretation to scriptural texts; on the other hand, it subordinates general hermeneutics to its own internal agenda of interpreting the meaning of the distinctive and "eccentric" subject matter of the Bible for the Christian community.

> In this sense, biblical hermeneutics is a *regional* hermeneutics in relation to philosophical hermeneutics. It may seem then that we sanction the subordination of biblical hermeneutics to philosophical hermeneutics in treating it as an applied hermeneutics.
> But it is precisely in treating theological hermeneutics as a hermeneutics applied to a species of texts—the biblical texts—that we bring to light an

opposite relationship between the two hermeneutics. Theological hermeneutics presents qualities so original that the relation progressively reverses itself, theological hermeneutics finally subordinating philosophical hermeneutics as its own *organon* [theoretical tool] . . . nothing will make the "eccentric" character of theology more apparent than the effort to "apply" the general categories of hermeneutics to it.[45]

Theological hermeneutics at the first stage seeks to display the full range of potential meanings that can be attributed to the text. But without objective standards (like authorial intention or historical background) to guide this display, how is the interpreter at the second stage to adjudicate which potential meanings are congruous with the text's sense and which are not? As Ricoeur asks, "Lacking the power to summon up the intention of the writer, is it not the reader's preference that ultimately makes the decision" concerning the text's meaning?[46] Ricoeur's answer is to borrow from Monroe Beardsley's *Aesthetic* two related interpretive guidelines: the principle of "fittingness" and the principle of "plenitude."[47] The principle of plenitude is especially operative at the first stage as the rule that opens up the text to all its possible connotations, allowing the text to mean all that it *can* mean; the principle of fittingness, on the other hand, restricts the range of connotations in the text by an appeal to the congruence between these connotations and the text's subject matter. While a final criteriology for verifying one reading over another cannot be produced, Ricoeur suggests that "hermeneutical rules of thumb" or a "logic of probability" can be invoked to adjudicate interpretive disputes at the level of explanation. "[I]f it is true that there is always more than one way of construing a text, it is not true that all interpretations are equal. The text presents a limited field of possible constructions. . . . It is always possible to argue for or against an interpretation, to confront interpretations, to arbitrate between them and to seek agreement, even if this agreement remains beyond our immediate reach."[48]

In principle, as Barth also observed, any explanatory resource can be used to guide the interpretive process. Ricoeur would agree with Augustine's observations in *De Doctrina Christiana* that the Christian exegete should make ready use of "all branches of heathen learning" in order to

---

[45]Ricoeur, "Philosophical Hermeneutics and Biblical Hermeneutics," 321-22.

[46]Paul Ricoeur, *The Rule of Metaphor: Multi-Disciplinary Studies of the Creation of Meaning in Language*, trans. Robert Czerny, Kathleen McCloughlin, and John Costello (Toronto: University of Toronto Press, 1975) 94.

[47]Ibid., 90-100.

[48]Paul Ricoeur, *Interpretation Theory: Discourse and the Surplus of Meaning* (Fort Worth: Texas Christian University Press, 1976) 79.

further the understanding of Scripture.[49] The value of historical criticism, for example, lies in its methodological return to the "minimal events" or historical "occasions" that gave rise to the Bible's literary compositions.[50] As we have seen, Ricoeur's hermeneutical focus is on the originary discourse of the Christian community's most basic testimony to the event of the Word of God; historical criticism enables the archaeological work necessary for uncovering the layers of tradition that transmit memories of the events that founded the early church and its witness. In conjunction with literary theory's facility for accessing the modes of discourse that later shaped and codified the church's witness, historical criticism performs the indispensable task of diachronically revealing the primal testimonies to the historylike event of God's communication to humankind within the *Sitz im Leben* of the early Christian community.[51] The danger in historical criticism, however, is that it may stop at the level of tradition-history analysis and not press on to ask the more properly hermeneutical question: what is the *meaning* of these different literary strata in combination with other strata from different times and places in the context of the final, redacted canonical text as a whole? That is, once the text's diachronic heterogeneity is recognized, what is the meaning of the text as a synchronic and intertextual whole irreducible to the sum of its historico-literary parts?

Here Ricoeur's criticism of historical criticism is analogous to Barth's. Ricoeur maintains that historical criticism's failure to address the issue of intertextuality stems from its affinities with, and antecedents in, philosophical historicism, in which the meaning of any human expression (textual or otherwise) can be explained by explicating the relevant factors (political, sociological, and so forth) that obtained during the time and at the place in which the expression was made.[52] No interpretive strategy, however, even one as scientifically rigorous as that which characterizes historical criticism, is "methodologically innocent"[53] of basic presuppositions concerning what does and does not count as the relevant criteria for understanding texts. What solitary historical-critical study of the Bible

---

[49]Augustine, *On Christian Doctrine,* in *Great Books of the Western World,* trans. J. F. Shaw, ed. R. M. Hutchins, vol. 18 (Chicago: Encyclopedia Britannica, Inc., 1952) 655.

[50]Paul Ricoeur, "From Proclamation to Narrative," *Journal of Religion* 64 (1984): 501-12.

[51]Paul Ricoeur, "Esquisse de conclusion," in *Exégèse et Herméneutique: Parole de Dieu,* ed. Xavier Léon Dufour (Paris: Editions du Seuil, 1971) 291 [my translation].

[52]Ricoeur, "Du conflict à la convergence des méthodes en exégèse biblique," in *Exégèse et Herméneutique,* 35-46.

[53]Ricoeur, "Esquisse de conclusion," 285.

gives us is not a real *understanding* of the biblical texts in the totality of their meaning for today, but only (though this is important) an *explanation* of what these texts might have meant given their historical circumstances. If the historical critic argues that her method affords both a historical explanation *and* a contemporary understanding, she commits a "genetic fallacy" that effectively eclipses an understanding of the text's full range of meanings as a composite whole by explaining the text's meaning solely on the basis of its connection to historical events.

Ricoeur argues that the basic problem with historical criticism is that it cannot account for the phenomenon of *intertextuality:* "The work of meaning through which one text in referring to another text both displaces this other text and receives from it an extension of meaning."[54] The use of discourse analysis in the Bible, however, does attend to the *"fête du sens"*[55] that results from the simultaneous juxtaposition of individual texts from different times and places. It examines how the text's sometimes harmonious, sometimes competing modes of discourse erect an open but ruled network of intersignifications in which the text's individual components both set aside and preserve their respective meanings in relation to other components in the overall text.

Ricoeur's point is that the explanatory moment must pass through the "archaeology" of the Bible's precanonical traditions in order to explain better how the different modes of discourse in the text's final, canonical form modulate the community's originary testimonies. At the explanatory level, the study of the text's final form is the end point or "teleology" of theological hermeneutics: the examination of the function of intertextuality (on the level of the text) or polysemy (on the level of the word) in a semantic study of biblical discourse. In the act of interpretation and reading, all the various forms of biblical discourse (whether they be narratives, prescriptions, hymns, prophecies, and so on) work together to enable the text's transfer from its original *Sitz im Leben* to a new *Sitz im Wort* in which the reality and identity of the divine life are now given in language.[56] As Barth also maintained, the original and naive construal of the text's overall meaning vis-à-vis its forms of discourse is now more rigorously examined, in the moment of explanation, with the aid of historical criticism and, more important, theological-literary readings of the biblical witness.

---

[54]Paul Ricoeur, "The Bible and the Imagination," in *The Bible as a Document of the University,* ed. Hans Dieter Betz (Chico CA: Scholars Press, 1981) 53.

[55]Ricoeur, "Contribution d'une réflexion sur le langage à une théologie de la parole," in *Exégèse et Herméneutique,* 314.

[56]Paul Ricoeur, "Time and Narrative in the Bible: Toward a Narrative Theology," Sarum Lectures, Oxford University, 1980, 1:1-8.

In the third moment for Barth, the bridge is crossed from explication to application, from *sensus* to *usus*. The expositor, however, does not put the Scripture to her use, because it is Scripture that "uses" her. We do not appropriate or assimilate Scripture; it appropriates us. "Instead of making use of Scripture at every step, it is Scripture itself which uses us—the *usus scripturae* in which *scriptura* is not object but subject, and the hearer and reader is not subject but object."[57] Barth's reversal of user and used, subject and object, is a defense of the freedom of the Word of God—to guard it against becoming a known entity that can be easily pressed into the service of the contemporary situation. For this reason, Barth had little patience with the correlation theologies of his time (such as those of Tillich and Bultmann) that regarded the scriptural Word as an answer to our most pressing existential questions and concerns. *Applicatio* does not mean "the adaptation of the Word of God to the service of this man. It is not the case that the exposition of Holy Scripture must finally issue in the answering of the so-called burning questions of the present day, that if possible it will acquire meaning and force as it is able to give an illuminating answer to the questions of the present generation."[58]

Whenever an authentic encounter occurs between interpreter and text, whenever the act of appropriation involves the submission of the interpreter's presuppositions and questions to the scriptural subject matter, then the possibility exists for contemporaneity between the interpreter and the biblical referent, Jesus Christ. "Because the Word of God meets us in the form of the scriptural word, assimilation means the contemporaneity, homogeneity and indirect identification of the reader and hearer of Scripture with the witness of revelation."[59] The moment of appropriation is the culmination of Barth's three-step hermeneutical method insofar as it accomplishes the direct encounter between the subject of the message proclaimed, Jesus Christ, and the object of the message's address, the interpreter.

Yet, the theological issue of how a historical person like Jesus of Nazareth can be decisively significant in the present has remained a difficult problem since the rise of historical consciousness during the Enlightenment. As Gotthold Ephraim Lessing put it, an ugly ditch separates the Jesus of history and our present-day context. But for Barth, Lessing's ugly ditch between past and present, Jesus and us, is bridged by the power of the biblical kerygma to place us into a concrete, spiritual relationship with the living Christ identified in the biblical narratives. Lessing's quandary is answered in the Christ-event. Barth solves (or, perhaps better, dis-

---

[57]Barth, *Church Dogmatics* 1:2, 738.

[58]Ibid.

[59]Ibid., 736.

solves) Lessing's problem by shifting the debate away from technical terms such as *historical facts* and *necessary truths* to the level of an existential dilemma: are we moderns willing to risk a transformative encounter with the Jesus identified as the Christ in the biblical texts, regardless of whether we think such an encounter is technically feasible? Hence, the real force of Lessing's question is felt by all of us who fear a miracle, who fear a final appropriation *by* the biblical Word *of* us in the unified process of biblical interpretation. Lessing's question concerning historical distance is really a pseudoproblem, argues Barth, that fades before the possibility of actual contemporaneity between us and Christ in the moment of encounter with the subject of the scriptural message. "The movement of flight into Lessing's problem is unnecessary. In and with the overcoming of the real and spiritual problem of the relationship between Jesus Christ and us, the technical problem of the relationship between then and there and the now and here is also soluble and has in fact been solved."[60] The apogee of Barth's theological hermeneutic is reached in the final moment of appropriation because it is here that the believing exegete is brought into a real and living relationship with the Christ narrated in the biblical texts.

The hermeneutical circle continues for Ricoeur as understanding follows an arc from a preunderstanding of the whole, to the testing of that understanding against the parts, to a reunderstanding of the whole in which the interpreter risks a divestiture of his sovereign self-consciousness in the light of the imaginative world that the text reveals. Now that an explanatory reading of the text's modes of discourse has been accomplished through historical and literary criticism, an existential appropriation of the biblical world refracted in these modes of discourse is demanded. For Ricoeur, the intersection between the world configured by the text and the world of the reader is the work of appropriation or mimesis 3. The emplotted world of the Bible refigures the reader's lived experience in time and space so that the text's specific temporality and historicality can now become ours in the act of reading, the act of appropriation. Scripture communicates to us the "inchoate narrative" or "untold story" that makes sense of our broken experience of the world; the text offers us a storied world that can "tell" our potential stories by uncovering the hidden meaning of human existence in time and history. In this way our vision of reality becomes refigured by the text's when we are willing to allow the text's world to structure and emplot our own world. As Barth queried, so does Ricoeur: will the reader risk exchanging his own self-understanding for the new understanding of the reader that the text projects? In theological parlance, will the reader become a "disciple" of the new mode of existence at the heart of the biblical understanding of reality? "But the matter of the text only becomes my own if I disappro-

[60]Ibid., 4:1, 293.

priate myself, in order to let the matter of the text be. Then I exchange the *me, master* of itself, for the *self, disciple* of the text."[61]

The essence of appropriation is the intersection of the world of the biblical texts and the world of the reader. The traversal of understanding through each stage reaches its fulfillment in this mediation between the text's vision and our vision. The text-world is a semantic window through which reality is refigured as a possible reality (mimesis 3) that I may explore and inhabit by letting go of my original prefigured view of things (mimesis 1). The text-world initiates an "iconic augmentation"[62] in which Scripture's nonostensive references actually increase the being of things by allowing us to see something *as* something else; in this we encounter the "revelation of a real more real than ordinary reality" by the indirect and suggestive modes of reference characteristic of the biblical witness.[63]

In the final moment of appropriation the disciplines of general hermeneutics and biblical hermeneutics both converge and separate. Insofar as the biblical subject matter is discoverable like any other textual subject matter, there is convergence; yet insofar as this subject matter is only found in the distinctive medium of the biblical witness, there is divergence. The biblical text-world qua text is understood as one text among many; but the biblical text-world as a medium for the Word of God can finally only be appropriated as the unique announcement of the New Being in our midst. In this appropriation, the reader discovers in the world of the text a restructuring of his or her own understanding of God, self, and world; and in this new understanding comes a sort of joy and liberation, even new life.

The moment of appropriation in Barth and Ricoeur initiates the fusion between the world of the text and the world of the reader. Passing through stages one and two, the reader finds that the text-world's appeal to rethink reality in line with the text's view of things sets free a once-lost, but now critically tempered naiveté toward the biblical subject matter. Barth speaks of the power of the biblical world to stimulate a "critical naiveté" on the part of its readers,[64] while Ricoeur notes the possibility of a "second naiveté" for modern interpreters who are willing to reappropriate critically the great biblical symbols of the past for the present.[65] When

---

[61]Paul Ricoeur, "Phenomenology and Hermeneutics," in *Hermeneutics and the Human Sciences,* ed. and trans. John B. Thompson (Cambridge: Cambridge University Press, 1981) 113.

[62]Ricoeur, *Interpretation Theory,* 40-43; idem, "Time and Narrative," 1:80-82, and *Rule of Metaphor,* 189.

[63]Ricoeur, *Interpretation Theory,* 40-43.

[64]Barth, *Church Dogmatics* 4:2, 479.

[65]Ricoeur, *Symbolism of Evil,* 351.

readers have passed through (but not beyond) the moments of original understanding and explanation, Barth and Ricoeur maintain that a full-orbed hermeneutic frees a new attentive openness to the witness of the Bible to a Word mediated by (but not reducible to) the biblical words. Ricoeur puts this point well in speaking of the dialectic between "the believer in the hermeneut when he is faithful to the community, and . . . the hermeneut in the believer when he does his scientific work of exegesis. This is today the dual condition of modern man in whom struggles both a believer and an atheist; in the believer himself there confront one another an adult critic and a naive child who listen to the Word."[66]

Barth's and Ricoeur's text-immanent hermeneutics seek to be more thoroughly critical than historical exegesis not only because their hermeneutics question the basic presupposition of historical criticism—that the biblical world is intelligible on the basis of its original location in a world behind the text—but also because their hermeneutics seek to interpret the world or subject matter in front of the text as a world that can be contemporaneous with the world of the reader. Herein the interpreter is both "adult critic" and "naive child"—both methodologically rigorous in explaining the text's parts and Christianly innocent again in theologically and existentially appropriating the message of the text as a whole. On this issue our theologian and our philosopher demonstrate a fundamental affinity: the call for a mature naiveté toward the biblical world as the telos of theological hermeneutics points to the organic unity between understanding, explanation, and appropriation in interpretation. And in the labor of interpretation the reality that *precedes* me and *proceeds* to me from the text can become mine, as critic and believer, in the final moment of appropriation.

· The Problem of Personalism ·

Up to this point I have argued for three broad areas of convergence in Barth's and Ricoeur's theological hermeneutics. First, both thinkers maintain that interpretation is governed by the capacity of the biblical witness to mediate the Word of God to the reader. This Word is heard in the intertextual echoes that reverberate throughout the whole biblical saga, from the play of presence and absence in Mark that hearkens back to themes in wisdom literature in Ricoeur's hermeneutic, to the strong readings of the Levitical and Pauline typologies in Barth's hermeneutics. Second, Barth's and Ricoeur's related disagreements with Bultmann's hermeneutics are that the message of the biblical Word cannot be separated from the literary forms that frame this word. Bultmann's primary concern with the demythologized translatability of the biblical text-world compromises the hermeneutical exigency to display this world in its full-

---

[66]Paul Ricoeur, "The Critique of Religion," in *Philosophy of Paul Ricoeur*, 222.

ness through a sensitive study of its varied forms of discourse. And third, the display of the text-world follows a three-step method of understanding, explanation, and appropriation, in which the goal is to realize a critically won naiveté toward the *Sitz im Wort* of the world in front of the biblical texts—a world, according to Barth and Ricoeur, that is identifiable neither with the historical conditions nor the authorial intentions behind the biblical texts, nor with the seemingly open-ended dissemination of meaning within these texts.

Barth's and Ricoeur's hermeneutics bear affinities in these three areas, but their positions are very different in other aspects, indicating how problematic a mediation of their respective hermeneutics can be. Though they offer related arguments for the primacy of the biblical text-world in interpretation, as we will see Barth's "world" is often very different from Ricoeur's, and vice versa. Can it be that our theologian and philosopher formulate such different understandings of the content of the text-world that a mediation of these differences is impossible, thus rendering a theological hermeneutic indebted to their respective insights fundamentally flawed because it contains two basically opposed versions of what exactly the text-world in question is?

In the postwar era Martin Heidegger argued that we now view the world as a megamachine—a standing reserve of stockpiled energy to be exploited for its technological power. The essence of the modern worldview is one with the essence of modern technology: the destiny of humankind is to dominate the natural order and use it as a giant power station so that it will yield its energy resources.[67] Since Heidegger's observation theological writers have become acutely aware of the Christian tradition's complicity in the creation of this mind-set—a mind-set that has fueled the global ecological crisis by reducing nature to a manipulable standing reserve. In pitting humankind against nature where nature is pictured as something "lower" or "other," historic Christianity has set the stage for our treatment of the natural world as an exploitable energy bank. As a result, many contemporary theologians and exegetes are articulating new ecologically sensitive theories of nature and creation in order to discharge Christianity's debt for causing (at least partially) the environmental crisis.

Jürgen Moltmann's *God in Creation*, the second installment in his developing systematic theology, develops a nonmechanistic, integrated theology of nature that envisions God as Spirit, humankind as a totality of body and soul, and nature as the place where the Sabbath God of the Bible rests and plays with all living things.[68] Walter Brueggemann's *The*

---

[67]Martin Heidegger, "The Question concerning Technology," in *The Question concerning Technology and Other Essays* (New York: Harper & Row, 1977) 3-35.

[68]Jürgen Moltmann, *God in Creation: A New Theology of Creation and the Spirit of God* (New York: Harper & Row, 1985).

Land maintains that the central biblical theme of the divine gift of the fertile land to Israel challenges the mainstream Christian theological assumption that the God-human relationship is the Bible's primary concern.[69] And H. Paul Santmire in *The Travail of Nature* suggests replacing the Christian tradition's preference for a Platonic "metaphor of ascent"—in which nature is the bottom step in humanity's upward march to disembodied bliss with God—with a "metaphor of fecundity" where the material world is viewed as the good earth, blessed by God, because it supplies and sustains all life.[70]

In these works and others, the opening creation hymn of Genesis remains the basic documentary source for thinking about ecological issues in Christian theology today. Yet Genesis 1 has had an ambiguous legacy in Christian theologies of creation, as this text is often read as picturing God and humanity over and against nature, not with nature. The need continues for fresh ecological readings of the inaugural Genesis creation story. In what follows I will explore Paul Ricoeur's cosmological hermeneutic of Genesis 1-2 in relation to the more anthropocentric interpretation of the creation accounts characteristic of Barth's exegesis.

Ricoeur's thought begins with the recognition that the Bible is a complicated intertext with competing modes of discourse, not a stable book structured by a uniform anthropological concern. As we have seen, while prophetic and narrative discourse emphasize God's covenantal relationship with Israel and the church in history through the Word of God, wisdom and hymnic discourse focus on the divine life's participation in all living things through the rhythms of the cosmos, the cycles of the seasons, the mystery of organic regeneration. The Bible is full of variety, and any exegetical or theological attempt to short-circuit this variety with a narrow concern for the human person as the sole focus of divine activity does a disservice to the multifaceted world projected by the various modes of discourse within the Bible.

Ricoeur maintains that the world of the biblical texts has a global horizon with a full ensemble of human and nonhuman motifs:

> [T]he world of the text . . . is here a question of a world, in the sense of a
> global horizon, of a totality of meanings, [in which] there is no privilege
> whatsoever for an instruction addressed to the individual person, and in
> general none for personal aspects, in the form of I-Thou or in general in
> the relation of man to God. The biblical world has aspects which are cosmic
> (it is a creation), which are communitarian (it speaks of Israel and the King-
> dom of God), and which are personal. Man is reached through a multi-

---

[69]Walter Brueggemann, *The Land: Place as Gift, Promise, and Challenge in Biblical Faith* (Philadelphia: Fortress Press, 1977).

[70]H. Paul Santmire, *The Travail of Nature: The Ambiguous Ecological Promise of Christian Theology* (Philadelphia: Fortress Press, 1985).

plicity of dimensions which are as much cosmological and historical and worldly as they are anthropological, ethical, and personal.[71]

This is a remarkable statement in light of Western theology's consistent understanding of nature as a kind of stage upon which the special salvation-drama between God and humanity is played out. Ricoeur finds this privileging of the human over the nonhuman at odds, however, with the first-order data given in Scripture, irrespective of what Christian theology has said on the subject.

An example of Ricoeur's cosmological hermeneutic can be found in his distinctive interpretation of the first creation account in the Book of Genesis. In an important but rarely discussed article entitled "Sur l'exégèse de Genèse 1, 1–2, 4a,"[72] he argues that Christian exegetes like von Rad and Werner H. Schmidt who emphasize the salvation of the human in Genesis miss the cosmic dimensions of the text, which stresses the creation of the world, not the beginning of salvation-history. A literary analysis of the P creation saga shows it to be a self-contained theological work that sustains a dialectic between the creation of the world and the creation of humankind; historical-critical exegesis, on the other hand, considers it to be an integral prelude to the Yahwist's salvation-history scheme in the Pentateuch—a prelude that subordinates the early Genesis cosmological musings to the soteriological concerns of later chapters.

A close literary reading of Genesis 1, however, militates against this traditional *Heilsgeschichte* approach to the creation story. Structurally, the text is characterized by a series of oppositions: between the primordial, brooding, mobile Ruah of the first two verses and the discursive, speaking, creating Elohim of the subsequent verses; and between the planets-sky pole and the human-earth pole. These tensions are mediated by the theme of separation. Initially, God ordains the heavenly lights to divide night from the day and summer from winter; later, God commands the earth and the waters to be agents of discrimination by bringing forth fauna and foliage after their own kind. The sun, moon, and stars are commissioned to separate night from day and equip the earth to bring forth all plant and animal life. The heavens and earth, then, serve as God's special mediators in the creation process. Ricoeur even calls them the "words of God,"[73] because it is they, not human beings, that are the divinely chosen instruments for ordering and generating life in its fullness: nature governs the rhythms of the seasons and the proliferation of living things on the earth.

Ricoeur takes issue with the traditional exegesis of these accounts, which claims human creation as the climax of the narrative. The creation

---

[71]Ricoeur, "Philosophy and Religious Language," 81–82.

[72]In *Exégèse et Herméneutique,* 67–84.

[73]Ibid., 81.

of the cosmos is not simply the buildup to the creation of the human, but rather the hymn's cosmological counterpoint to the soteriological theme. Hence, creation "marks the limits of man, the milieu which precedes and envelops him, the universe which comprises him."[74] The creation song in Genesis 1 contains many themes and counter-themes, and more than one crescendo; the natural order is the medium of humanity's existence, not merely a subtheme in the creation song. Far from being merely the incidental backdrop to this story about human origins, the natural environment is the all-enveloping, life-sustaining order that undergirds and nourishes the fragile human species. According to this reading, creation, quite literally, is the divinely appointed "ecosystem" or "biosphere" established for the maintenance of all life. So rather than serving as the apex of God's creative activity, the creation of humankind in Genesis 1 is but one theme—albeit a very important theme—within the hymn of cosmic celebration that inaugurates the story of the Bible.

In all his biblical writings, Ricoeur's concern is to wed theology and exegesis, to correlate theological reflection and the analysis of the first-order discourse of the church's sacred texts. His theological and structural reading of Genesis 1 is a good case in point: if Scripture's opening chapters announce a parity between the creation of humankind and the creation of nature, then Christian soteriology and cosmology must labor to assign a balanced emphasis to the question of human salvation and the status of the nonhuman order within the divine design. While the Yahwist's narrative concerning God and Israel dominates the Pentateuch, Ricoeur concludes that the cosmic thematic in wisdom and hymnic discourse—a thematic present at the outset of the Yahwist's salvation-history in the Priestly song of creation in Genesis 1 and carried through by Qoheleth and Job—is the necessary counterpoint to the Old Testament's soteriological theme. Ricoeur contends that

> it is the Yahwist faith which superimposes the problematic of salvation onto that of creation. The cosmic statements are also placed in the same category as the soteriological statements. . . . It can be asked, with an exegete like J.-P. Audet, if wisdom is not older and already contemporary with the totality of Hebrew Scripture and if it itself does not envelop soteriology. . . . In furnishing a counter-accent to the matter of the creation of man, [Genesis 1] announces an interest in the cosmic thematic that is not exhausted in the message concerning salvation.[75]

Ricoeur notes that the history-of-traditions approach of exegetes like von Rad and Schmidt (and we could add the names of G. E. Wright and Bernhard Anderson as well) subordinates cosmology to anthropology by

---

[74]Ibid., 82.

[75]Ibid.

reading the Bible in reverse, as it were, from the stories of the Exodus and Sinai backward to the cosmic speculations of the Priestly creation story.

Another and more familiar exponent of this person-centered approach is Karl Barth. Barth would likely find Ricoeur's "global horizon" to be too diffuse because it does not acknowledge that even the Bible's teachings about the world are essentially teachings about God's relationship to the human person. For Barth, the Word of God is primarily concerned with God and humankind; it speaks *directly* to this relationship and only *indirectly* to those dimensions of the biblical world—the cosmos and nature—that Ricoeur places on an equal footing with the Bible's teaching about humankind. For Barth, God's grace toward humankind is the proper and particular focus of the biblical message. Even in the doctrine of creation, the first issue is humankind, not the created order. "Because man is the creature whose relation to God is revealed to us in the Word of God, he is the central object of the theological doctrine of creation"; and he adds, *"In practice, the doctrine of creation means anthropology—the doctrine of man"* (emphasis mine).[76]

Although Barth's theology ranges over all the many topics within the Christian and humanist traditions—from creation to the eschaton, from Judas to Mozart—it always operates with the concern to let God in Christ speak freely to the human person. His early critics thought Barth's dialectical theology would be unable to make a place for humankind in his system, but his mature theology actually accords theological anthropology a very prominent place in his overall dogmatics: theology and anthropology are interrelated issues for the later Barth, a kind of "theanthropology,"[77] as he once put it.

Even though he eschews the anthropocentrism of liberal Protestant theology, which elevated human religion (according to Barth) as its object of study, Barth's own theology is always directed to the question of human salvation and God's special covenant with humankind. Even his celebrated concern with the Godhood of God ("Let God be God") is consistently associated with God's gracious relationship to the human. Adjusting his earlier emphasis on the Wholly Other's isolation from humanity, he says: "But did it not appear to escape us that the deity of the living God . . . found its meaning and power only in the context of his history and dialogue with man?"[78] In this quotation, Barth's person-centered bias is apparent: the axis of the biblical world turns on God's special covenantal relationship with humankind. But can we really say

---

[76]Barth, *Church Dogmatics* 3:2, 3.

[77]Busch, *Karl Barth*, 424.

[78]Karl Barth, *The Humanity of God,* trans. John Newton Thomas (Atlanta: John Knox Press, 1960) 45.

that the meaning of God's deity and life is found *only* in God's dialogue with *us*? Are theology and anthropology as interrelated as Barth indicates?

While Ricoeur reads the Genesis creation passages as maintaining a tensive parity between cosmology and soteriology, Barth argues that creation is but the "framework" or "theatre" or "external basis" for God's primary concern with human salvation.[79] Creation has no autonomous basis or independent meaning apart from its place as the sphere in which the history of salvation is worked out. In Barth's now-classic formula, creation is the external basis of the convenant, and the convenant is the internal basis of creation: the whole created order has been established for the sake of the covenant between God and humanity.[80] Barth acknowledges that biblical writings other than Genesis 1 balance the role of humankind in creation with an emphasis on the created order itself (he mentions Psalm 104 and Job 38 as examples). Nevertheless, as he reads it, Scripture's first pages yield an unvarnished anthropocentric view of the cosmos that accords to humankind the privilege of being the very center of, and the basis for unity within, the whole of creation. "But the knowledge of man's existence and being and right and honor in the center of creation, and therefore the knowledge of the unity of everything created, is no small matter. There can certainly be no question of a more naive and direct anthropocentricity."[81] Barth concludes that the "naive and direct anthropocentricity" of the first two chapters of Genesis is a clear and obvious fact of the biblical world that is available to any discerning reader.[82]

James Gustafson correctly designates Barth's thought in this regard as "anthropocentric" (certainly an ironic label given Barth's disagreements with Protestant liberalism on precisely this issue, though for different reasons), because while "Jesus Christ is the center of Barth's theology," his "theology sustains [an] excessive focus on the salvation of persons."[83] Gustafson's work counters the long-standing consensus in the Christian

---

[79]This anthropocentric bias in Barth's doctrine of creation is examined by Santmire in "The Triumph of Personalism: Karl Barth and Teilhard de Chardin," chap. 8 in *The Travail of Nature*: "[Barth's] theology is fundamentally a theology of personal being, of God and humanity, and that is virtually all. Everything else in the visible creation, as far as he is concerned, is subservient to, and instrumental for, that theme" (155).

[80]See Barth, *Church Dogmatics* 3:1, §41, 42-328.

[81]Ibid., 21.

[82]Ibid., 23.

[83]James M. Gustafson, *Ethics from a Theocentric Perspective*, 2 vols. (Chicago: University of Chicago Press, 1984) 2:28.

tradition, a consensus shared by Barth, that God's primary and proper concern is the salvation and welfare of the human species. For Gustafson, like Ricoeur, the divine benevolence includes, but is not especially directed toward, human flourishing.

In fairness to Barth, it should be noted that his theology of creation was understandably symptomatic of his time—a time when the concern for nature vis-à-vis the environmental crisis had not been recognized. I am not, then, anachronistically criticizing Barth for his failure to develop an ecologically sound theory of nature, but for concentrating his theology almost solely on the God-human relationship. His focus limits the world of nature to a theatre for the playing out of this relationship within the economy of salvation. Yet Barth's devaluation of nature was not unique to his time, even as Ricoeur's substantive concern for the natural order in his hermeneutics is, I suspect, a reflection of the post-1960s awareness of the ecological crisis. The paradigm shift in contemporary theology on the nature issue—creation is now often viewed as a third datum alongside God and humanity to be included in theological reflection—occurred in the time period between Barth's dogmatics and Ricoeur's mature writing. As important as this difference between Barth and Ricoeur is, both thinkers' theologies of creation should be read not only as the products of their biblical exegesis but also as reflections of the cultural sensibilities of their time.

Be this as it may, it does seem that Barth's controlling interest to portray the divine life as "God for man" limits in effect the "full display," as Ricoeur says, of the biblical world with its nonanthropological coordinates. Though Barth and Ricoeur offer related arguments for the primacy of the textual world in interpretation, Ricoeur's world is actually quite different from Barth's because it contains a global horizon that seeks to maintain a balance between the many components of experience, between the human and the nonhuman orders within the divine care. Ricoeur's cosmologically sensitive reading of the Genesis creation accounts is a novel and successful revision of the Barthian stress on the covenantal history of God and humanity in Genesis 1-2. By maintaining that nature is the divine mediator in the creation and fulfillment of humankind, not a way station for the march of the covenant through history, Ricoeur upholds a vision of the natural world that echoes the cadences of the Bible's initial creation hymn, "And behold, it was very good." I find that Ricoeur's hermeneutic offers a persuasive critique of Barth's position: Barth's "theanthropology" narrowly shrinks the biblical world because it too sharply focuses on the God-human relationship at the expense of other modalities within this textual world.

• The Problem of Christocentrism •

This initial problem between Barth and Ricoeur refracts a related disagreement. While they formally stand together in according the biblical world a primacy in interpretation, Barth and Ricoeur interpret the material content of this world differently. According to Barth, the subject matter of the Bible is plainly Jesus Christ—the son of the God who is gracious to sinful humanity. While the Bible says many things in different ways, its coherent center is the Word of God definitely identified as Jesus Christ. "The Bible says all sorts of things . . . but it says in truth only one thing: the name of Jesus Christ."[84] In the act of observation, the interpreter follows the arrow of the text's sense to its reference; and, in principle, any interpretation should disclose the reality of Jesus Christ as the determining and controlling subject matter of the whole biblical witness in spite of the plurality of other diverse themes and subthemes within the Bible. Barth's mediation of the general hermeneutic/biblical hermeneutic dialectic is clear on this issue: "In conclusion, we must again emphasize that in taking this line biblical, theological hermeneutics is not claiming for itself a mysterious special privilege. The object of the biblical texts is quite simply the name Jesus Christ, and these texts can be understood only when understood as determined by this object. But this insight is not a privilege of theologians. It could also be an insight of the interpreter as such."[85] In this passage Barth does not mean to suggest that general hermeneutics have faithfully located as primary the Christ-referent in their exegesis, but rather that there is no textual reason why they should not be able to do so, since the biblical records consistently bear out this reference.

Christian systematic theology maintains a thoroughgoing christological concentration in keeping with the results of biblical criticism. As he states in a retrospective article, Barth regards his strong intrabiblical conviction on this point to be a repudiation of the "eggshells of philosophical systematics" that so plagued his earlier thought—as well as the general course of modern theology.[86] "The positive factor in the new development was this: in these years I had to learn that Christian doctrine, if it is to merit its name and if it is to build up the Christian church in the world as she must needs be built up, has to be exclusively and conclusively the doctrine of Jesus Christ—of Jesus Christ as the living Word of God spoken to us men."[87] Twenty years later Barth put it another way, arguing that the message of the Bible for modern-day theology can be summed up by the formula he had learned as a young man from the Blumhardt brothers' theology of hope: "Jesus is Victor."[88] Scripture's *Christus Victor*

---

[84]Barth, *Church Dogmatics* 1:2, 720.

[85]Ibid., 727.

[86]See Karl Barth, "How My Mind Has Changed in This Decade: Part Two," *Christian Century* 101 (July 1984): 684-86 (reprint from 20 September 1939 issue).

[87]Ibid., 684.

[88]See Barth, *Church Dogmatics* 4:3.1, §69.3, 165-274.

motif obligates the dogmatic theologian to rethink and recast all the major *topoi* of the Christian heritage in line with the triumphant person and work of Jesus Christ. Barth maintains, however, that this process of christological theologizing is always a supple and elastic handling of the clear biblical witness to the living Christ rather than a rigid and arithmetical deduction of doctrines from a formal Christ-principle. In Barth's response to G. C. Berkouwer's critique of his theology,[89] he says that "christological thinking in this sense is a very different process from deduction from a given principle. I underline, however, that we are not dealing with a Christ-principle, but with Jesus Christ Himself as attested by Holy Scripture."[90]

Ricoeur's theological hermeneutic, on the other hand, operates with no such christological lodestar, and herein lies a major area of disagreement between the two thinkers. Ricoeur broadly defines the biblical world as a multiplicity of discourses and references that all project an imaginative ontology: a plurality of ways of being in the world that redescribes reality as the reality of the possible. For Barth, the world of the text is not an ensemble of imaginative variations on a *possible* reality; it projects, rather, the one and only *actual* reality of the living Christ who makes possible our obedience to the biblical witness. Ricoeur maintains, however, that the revelation to which the Bible witnesses—the revelation of another possible mode of existence than that to which we are accustomed— is never monolithic or uniform. "Instead of having to confront a monolithic concept of revelation . . . we encounter a concept of revelation that is pluralistic, polysemic, and at most analogical in form."[91]

Revelation is polyphonic, but the biblical text-world is not a cacophony for Ricoeur. Though revelation is varied, its multiple voices are coordinated by its consistent references to the divine life. "God talk . . . is at once the coordinator of these varied discourses and the index of their incompleteness."[92] According to Ricoeur, the biblical references to God and Christ unify Scripture's diverse literary forms into a coherent whole. But the stories about God and those about Christ cannot be collapsed into a single reference, be it theocentric of christocentric. In Ricoeur's parlance, the word *Christ* gives specific, historical "density" to the word *God* and protects the biblical God-referent from being merely an abstract, philosophical concept. Yet Christ can neither exhaust nor be completely identified with God, because the full identity of the biblical God escapes

---

[89]See G. C. Berkouwer, *The Triumph of Grace in the Theology of Karl Barth*, trans. Harry R. Boer (Grand Rapids MI: Wm. B. Eerdmans Publishing Co., 1956).

[90]Barth, *Church Dogmatics* 4:3.1, 174.

[91]Ricoeur, "Hermeneutic of Revelation," 75.

[92]Ricoeur, "Philosophy and Religious Language," 83.

even the character of Jesus Christ.[93] Scripture is radically intertextual with a plurality of divine references, to God and Christ, each of which mutually corrects and extends the meaning of the other.

There is no homogeneous referent to which all the discourse-specific theologies of Scripture are addressed. In one sense, the word *God* is the master referent that gathers up all the diverse forms of biblical discourse. Yet the God-referent of the Bible does not function in isolation from other referents, but is rather constituted by them. There can be, then, no closure to the hermeneutical quest for settling the question as to who God is or what God is like, because each biblical way of speaking "names God" according to its own nuanced vision of reality. As Lawgiver in the Psalms, Wisdom in the Sayings, and Jesus Christ in the Gospels, the divine life is defined according to the varied literary forms that make up the biblical text-world. Ricoeur, therefore, is opposed to a christocentric hermeneutic of Christian texts and doctrines that dislocates the integrity of the symbol of God in favor of the Christ symbol. "I will not hesitate to say that I resist with all my strength the displacement of the accent from God to Jesus Christ, which would be the equivalent of substituting one naming for another."[94] Scripture is not read, nor is doctrine formulated, with a christological concentration (nor any other single concentration) that would finally construe the different revelations of the Word of God as monolithic and not polysemic.

Barth, certainly, cannot fairly be charged with substituting Christ for God. Nevertheless, Ricoeur's point is well taken, namely that while a Barthian christocentric interpretation theory is consistent with *some* trajectories within Scripture and tradition, it also threatens hermeneutically to homogenize and thereby impoverish the rich diversity of the biblical world. This is a substantive hermeneutical conflict between the two thinkers: Barth's christocentric exegesis versus Ricoeur's polysemic model for reading the Bible. Formally speaking, Barth and Ricoeur do share prima facie a common three-step hermeneutical method—interpretation follows an arc from observation to explanation and finally to appropriation—but the issue of a christocentric versus polysemic hermeneutic sharpens the issue concerning what each thinker regards as the proper subject matter of this common method.

Barth and Ricoeur both understand that the inaugural moment in any adequate hermeneutic (be it general or biblical) is to "let the text speak" (Barth) or to "display the world of the text" (Ricoeur), while the explanatory moment looks to test what we have initially found against the text's individual parts, the parts that make up the naive "world" of our first guess or construal. The first step is to accord the text the full plenitude of

[93]Ibid.

[94]Paul Ricoeur, "Naming God," *Union Seminary Quarterly Review* 34 (1979): 224.

possible meanings that can reasonably be assigned to it, and the second step asks whether this assignment is adequate to the nature of the subject matter at hand. Ricoeur's problem with some Protestant exegetes such as von Rad, Bultmann, and Barth, however, is that they essentially forgo these first and second steps by arriving too quickly at what they consider to be the text's central message: salvation-history (von Rad), authentic existence (Bultmann), or Jesus Christ (Barth). Ricoeur would not, I think, disagree in principle with Barth's three-step exegetical method, but with the Swiss theologian's application of this method as a support for the christological foundation of his dogmatic theology. Ricoeur's guiding concern is to display the full text-world in all its semantic richness so that revelation is understood intertextually and polysemically. Barth's hermeneutical interest, on the other hand, is to show that revelation is always a predicate of the Christ-event, so that the whole Bible, even at the first step of observation, is read as having a sort of preestablished christocentric harmony. Though Barth and Ricoeur appear to share a common hermeneutical method, the overriding christological orientation of the former and the exegetical *fête du sens* openness of the latter lead to strikingly different theological construals of the nature of the biblical text-world.

It is not surprising, then, that such different hermeneutical postures lead to divergent theological positions. We can see this contrast in how Barth and Ricoeur handle the problem of evil. Initially, each thinker's starting point is similar. Both recognize that theology cannot offer a strictly logical answer to the problem of evil, but only a broken response to a dilemma in which the reality of evil and the nature of a loving and all-powerful God seem irreconcilable. Consequently, both thinkers return to the originary discourse concerning evil and God in the Bible to formulate their own respective intrabiblical theodicies. But here the similarity ends, because while Barth looks to the clear christological message of the Gospels and Paul in support of his position, Ricoeur accents the marginalized discourse of the Old Testament's wisdom writings for his.

Ricoeur's hermeneutic appropriates the action of *lament* in biblical wisdom discourse as a response to the problems of evil.[95] His thesis is that wisdom discourse provides an enabling response to the dilemma of innocent suffering that avoids the theoretical difficulties of traditional speculative theodicies. Instead of theoretical solutions to the problem of evil, Ricoeur offers the praxis of lamentation—cathartic indignation against unjustified suffering—as a viable response to evil beyond the failure of speculative solutions to the problem. Regarding the perennial complaint

---

[95]See Ricoeur, "Hermeneutic of Revelation," 85-90. Also see Paul Ricoeur, "Evil, A Challenge to Philosophy and Theology," *Journal of the American Academy of Religion* 53 (1985): 635-50.

"Why me?," Ricoeur writes: "The emotional response that the practical one calls forth as its necessary complement cannot be anything other than a catharsis of the emotions that nourish the lament and that transform it into complaint. . . . What I should like to do is consider Wisdom, with its philosophical and theological prolongations, as a spritual help in this work of mourning, aimed at a qualitative change in the lament and the complaint."[96] Only a theodicy that does not try intellectually to solve the riddle of unjust suffering, but offers a lived and practical way of being in light of the problem, can enable us to face adequately the eruption of evil in our experience.

Barth's christocentric response to the problem of evil—or radical nothingness, as he prefers—in *Church Dogmatics* 3:1 and 3:3 revisits the classical response to the issue: Jesus' death and resurrection promise all who suffer that they will experience victory over sin and evil. "Because Jesus is Victor, nothingness is routed and extirpated. . . . It is no longer to be feared."[97] Ricoeur does not take issue with Barth on the potential value of this triumphal message to heal and transform the sufferer, but he insists that this is not the Bible's only message on the subject. When all the different modes of discourse in the Bible are allowed to intermingle, different aspects of revelation come to the surface, so that the problem of evil is addressed from many different angles. One angle is certainly the christological perspective, while another is the catharsis of lament upheld by Israel's wise men and seers.

In a 1984 address in Chicago, Ricoeur set out his lament-based response to the problem of evil and questioned Barth's theodicy as bordering on a speculative and triumphalist solution to the problem. Barth's theodicy does not do justice to the suffering that refuses to be subsumed under any theology (even a theology of the cross) which suggests that evil has already been overcome.[98] For the lamenter, evil has not been dealt the final deathblow. The Hebrew Bible makes this point, a point that should be respected in its own right and not glossed over as a deficient antecedent to the christological answer to the problem of evil in the New Testament.

Unlike Barth, then, Ricoeur does not allow for a thoroughgoing christological hermeneutic of the Old Testament in which the message of wisdom discourse is forgotten and eclipsed by the gospel message of the New Testament. One reason for Ricoeur's rejection of a Barthian typological reading of the Old Testament is related to his general hermeneutical principle of intertextuality. All classic historical texts, the Bible included, re-

---

[96]Ricoeur, "Evil," 646.

[97]Barth, *Church Dogmatics* 3:3, 363.

[98]Published as Ricoeur, "Evil."

ceive their intelligibility from the literary crisscrossing of the text's different modes of discourse and corresponding referents. In essence, Barth's Christ-centered exegesis is faulty because it stops the working of the text on itself. It effectively results in a christological closure to the interworking of the Bible's heterogeneous texts on one another, thereby blinding the interpreter to the surplus of meaning that results from this overall dynamic process.

But another reason for Ricoeur's disagreement with Barth is strictly theological. As in general hermeneutics one text is meaningful only as it works on the body of texts that preceded it, so in theological hermeneutics the Word of God projected in the New Testament can speak only as it takes up into itself the mixed discourse of the Hebrew Scriptures. The implicit theological agenda behind Ricoeur's hermeneutical concern for the text's fullness of meaning is the presupposition that it is the dynamic unity between the Old Testament and the New—a unity that is theological as well as textual—that makes possible the mediation of the Word of God to the Christian community. "The New Testament receives its intelligibility from the transfiguration it works, in a way behind itself, on the mass of texts from which it arises. . . . I do not hesitate to say, therefore, along with James Barr and others, that the New Testament, separated from the Old, remains mute and unintelligible. . . . The story of Jesus 'makes sense' only at the intersection of the Old and New Testaments, which together form the great intertext of Christian faith."[99] As a philosopher of texts who labors to understand better the Christian faith, Ricoeur maintains that the New Testament receives its intelligibility not from typologically or christologically controlling the pluriformity of the Hebrew Bible's many modes of discourse and referents, but from transfiguring and reworking these diverse ways of speaking in light of the New Being that the Bible announces to its readers.

Consequently, an adequate Christian response to the theodicy problem must travel the long detour through the Old Testament's wisdom-based understanding of living with evil before it can begin to live and hope in the promised land of Christ's victory over evil. If the journey is to be successful, it must respect the model of lamentation in Job, Proverbs, and Lamentations as a viable answer to the problem. This answer should be regarded on its own terms and not typologically dismissed as yielding a protochristological sense that is more important, even more true, than its plain meaning. For Ricoeur, the praxis of lamentation is a needed, but forgotten, response to the mystery and misery of undeserved punishment and suffering in our time.

Ricoeur's point regarding the theodicy question, as we have seen with many other issues, is that interpretation is productive when all the Bible's

---

[99]Ricoeur, "Time and Narrative in the Bible," 1:52.

different modes of discourse are allowed to intermesh and work together to provide complex and ever-widening answers to the questions that provoke us. Such answers may be initially difficult to appreciate because they are as conflicting and diverse as are the biblical theologies and linguistic forms from which they emerge. In the long run, however, Ricoeur wagers that we will find these solutions more satisfying, because they are more attuned to the contradictory complexities that make up our human world and the nonsentient world around us.

THE NEW YALE THEOLOGY

Intratextual theology redescribes reality within the scriptural framework rather than translating Scripture into extrascriptural categories. It is the text, so to speak, which absorbs the world, rather than the world the text.[1]

The 1984 publication of George Lindbeck's important book *The Nature of Doctrine: Religion and Theology in a Postliberal Age* highlighted an emerging consensus among the theology faculty of Yale University and Divinity School. In the last fifteen years or so, much of the ferment in American biblical hermeneutics has been caused by four theologians at Yale—Hans Frei, Paul Holmer, George Lindbeck, and David Kelsey[2]—who have published a number of books and articles that have programmatically outlined a counterpoint to traditional academic and apologetic theologies.[3]

---

[1]George A. Lindbeck, *The Nature of Doctrine: Religion and Theology in a Postliberal Age* (Philadelphia: Westminster Press, 1984) 118.

[2]For Frei, see *The Eclipse of Biblical Narrative: A Study in Eighteenth and Nineteenth Century Biblical Narrative* (New Haven: Yale University Press, 1974); *The Identity of Jesus Christ: The Hermeneutical Bases of Dogmatic Theology* (Philadelphia: Fortress Press, 1975); "The 'Literal Reading' of the Biblical Narrative in the Christian Tradition: Does It Stretch or Will It Break," in Frank McConnell, ed., *The Bible and the Narrative Tradition* (New York: Oxford University Press, 1986) 36-77; and "An Afterword: Eberhard Busch's Biography of Karl Barth," in H.-Martin Rumscheidt, ed., *Karl Barth in Re-View: Posthumous Works Reviewed and Assessed* (Pittsburgh: Pickwick Press, 1981) 95-116. For Holmer, see *The Grammar of Faith* (New York: Harper & Row, 1978); and "Wittgenstein: 'Saying' and 'Showing,' " *Neue Zeitschrift für systematische Theologie und Religionsphilosophie* 22 (1980): 222-35. For Lindbeck, see *Nature of Doctrine*; "The Bible as Realistic Narrative" *Journal of Ecclesiastical Studies* 17 (1980): 81-85. For Kelsey, see *The Uses of Scripture in Recent Theology* (Philadelphia: Fortress Press, 1975); and "The Bible and Christian Theology," *Journal of the American Academy of Religion* 48 (1980): 385-402.

[3]In this chapter, however, I have not examined David Kelsey's thought in relation to his theological colleagues at Yale. The reason for this partly stems from constraints of space, but the more important factor is that Kelsey's theological work

The Yale theologians cooperatively are attempting to forge a biblical alternative to mainstream theological liberalism that eschews both confessionalism and fundamentalism. Along with the hermeneutical programs of Barth and Ricoeur, I find the Yale postliberal alternative to be a welcome development as it seeks to redirect the Christian community's vision back to its scriptural sources and to the Bible's distinctive, even unique, vision of reality.

While this biblical approach is much needed, I will suggest in this chapter that the so-called New Yale Theology[4] is not without its problems, chief of which stem from (a) confusion surrounding its notion of foundationalism, and (b) a failure to reconcile its intratextual hermeneutics with its relativist notion of truth. The difficulty is that the Yale theologians criticize liberal theologians for grounding their proposals on a philosophical foundation that compromises the free expression of the biblical witness; yet as I hope to show in commenting on Ricoeur's hermeneutic, even some who have been called liberal have sought to avoid basing their theological reflections on extrabiblical presuppositions. Another problem is that the precise meaning of the term foundationalism in the literature under question is difficult to pin down because, ironically, while the Yale school purports to be intratextually dependent on the Bible for its reflections, in fact it uses a variety of concepts and ideas from the other disciplines in order to clarify—if not actually to ground—its own postliberal theological proposals. In the final analysis, a major question

---

has been more descriptive, and less constructive, than that of his Yale associates, making a comparison of his systematic thought with theirs more difficult. While Kelsey's own work on Barth's hermeneutic in the *Uses of Scripture* has undergirded his colleagues' narrative approach to theology, and while he too highlights the Bible's special "logic" or "patterns," my sense is that Kelsey's theological vision is less intratextual and more pluralistic than that of his colleagues (see Kelsey's comments to this effect in "The Bible and Christian Theology").

[4]The phrase belongs to Brevard S. Childs in "The Canonical Approach and the 'New Yale Theology' " in *The New Testament as Canon: An Introduction* (Philadelphia: Fortress Press, 1984) 541-46. In this article his disagreements with Lindbeck et al. show that the "New Yale Theology" is not a homogeneous movement embracing all theological reflection at Yale. Consequently, my use of such terms as the Yale school and the Yale theologians in this chapter is not intended to convey the impression of a highly organized theological "camp" at Yale, but to underscore, in Childs's words, "a distinct family resemblance among several recent theological proposals stemming from Yale" (541).

For a critical discussion of George Lindbeck's recent work in the context of the "New Yale Theology," see the four articles by William C. Placher, Colman O' Neill, James J. Buckley, and David Tracy in "Review Symposium: Lindbeck's *The Nature of Doctrine*," *Thomist* 49 (1985): 392-472. Also see the two review articles by Charles M. Wood and Timothy P. Jackson in *Religious Studies Review* 11 (1985): 235-45.

regarding the Yale school remains unanswered: is the biblical world the sole theological determinant of what reality is, as the Yale theologians sometimes assert, or, as they also seem to indicate, is the biblical world simply one language-game (Lindbeck, Holmer) or literary picture (Frei) amidst other games and pictures, none of which has priority over any other?

The chapter is divided into two parts. In the first section I will outline the common and salient features of the Yale school under the headings "intratextual hermeneutics," "grammatical method," and "ad hoc apologetics"; in the second section I will offer some points of critique regarding this emerging theological "school."

• Intratextualism, Grammar, and Ad Hoc Apologetics •

The most distinctive theme of the Yale school is its emphasis on the narrated world of the biblical texts as the primary medium for theological reflection. Scripture is not a reference point alongside "common human experience"[5] or the "constructive imagination"[6] for doing theology, but the definitive source for all theological work.

Lindbeck makes this point in his organization of contemporary theological theories of religion and doctrine into three types. The cognitive type is identified with traditional Protestant and Catholic orthodoxy's emphasis on the propositional character of Christian truth-claims. The experiential-expressive type is identified with liberalism's focus on doctrines as nondiscursive objectifications of core religious experiences. Most of modern theology, from Schleiermacher to Tillich, is located under this paradigm. Lindbeck's own model, the cultural-linguistic approach—indebted both to Wittgenstein's notion of "grammar" and Geertz's idea of cultural "thick description"—argues instead that religions and doctrines provide authoritative, grammarlike rules shaped by the cultural and linguistic norms of particular religious communities. Religions and doctrines are primarily grammars of the faithful rather than compilations of truth-claims or thematizations of inner feelings. Specifically, church doctrines are the *regulae fidei* that are governed by a distinctive, scriptural "logic" (for example, God is trinitarian, Jesus is divine and human) that shapes the

---

[5]The notion that theology has not just one source (i.e. Scripture) but two (i.e. "Christian texts" and "common human experience") is argued by David Tracy in his liberal revisionist book *Blessed Rage for Order: The New Pluralism in Theology* (New York: Seabury Press, 1975) chap. 3.

[6]Gordon D. Kaufman argues that "theology is not properly understood either as primarily biblical exegesis or as the exposition of traditional dogma or doctrine. Christian theology is essentially *construction*—construction, as carefully as possible, of a Christian view of God" (Gordon D. Kaufman, *The Theological Imagination* [Philadelphia: Westminster Press, 1981] 272).

communal life of the Christian church. The task of theology, then, is primarily descriptive: to uncover the grammar that has always guided the church's experience and specify its applicability to particular theological problems and concerns.[7]

The Scriptures are the prevenient authoritative texts that instantiate the rules and grammar of the church in a rough, presystematic narrative framework. Theology does not look outside this scriptural framework to describe reality, but rather takes its cues from the world of the biblical texts to shape the imagination and life of the Christian community. While liberal (experiential-expressive) theology seeks to translate Scripture into contemporary idioms as symbolic of our common religious experiences, Lindbeck's cultural-linguistic approach accords the Bible the privilege of dictating to theology its own distinctive vision of the world in its own terms without regard to the translatability of this vision. "Intratextual theology redescribes reality within the scriptural framework rather than translating Scripture into extrascriptural categories. It is the text, so to speak, which absorbs the world, rather than the world the text."[8] Intratextual theology seeks to transform and define all reality according to the biblical world, while extratextual theology—be it propositional or experiential-expressive—looks to reinterpret the biblical world according to nonbiblical thought-systems in order to render Scripture more meaningful and relevant to the contemporary situation.

Frei's two books published in the mid-1970s on biblical hermeneutics (and a recent article on the same[9]) make this intratextual point with equal force. In *The Eclipse of Biblical Narrative*, Frei argues that the history of modern biblical criticism and theology is fundamentally flawed by its failure to embrace the narrated realities of the Bible for determining the structure and content of theological work. While ancient and Reformation scholars did theology according to internal criteria provided by the storied world of Scripture, post-Enlightenment theologians square theological claims with general, extrabiblical theories that dictate to the Christian community what can and cannot count as a valid theological claim. "General theory here dictates to, not to say overwhelms, exegesis and subject matter in the case of at least one kind of text [that is, biblical narratives]."[10]

In language later echoed by Lindbeck's above-noted comment that "Scripture is to absorb the world," Frei argues that modern liberal theology performed the "great reversal" in which "interpretation was a matter of fitting the biblical story into another world with another story rather

---

[7]Lindbeck, *Nature of Doctrine*, chaps. 1, 2.

[8]Ibid., 118.

[9]See Frei, " 'Literal Reading' of the Biblical Narrative," 36-77.

[10]Frei, *Identity of Jesus Christ*, xvi.

than incorporating that world into the biblical story."[11] As Frei noted in the preface and introduction to *Eclipse*, his hermeneutics on this point have been influenced by Erich Auerbach's literary criticism of the Bible and other forms of epic literature. Frei agrees with Auerbach that the Bible functions as a realistic novel that impresses its narrative vision of reality onto us through the subtle interplay of character and incident in the stories it recounts. Frei's biblical hermeneutics closely echo Auerbach's demonstration of the "tyrannical authority" of the Old Testament and its insistence "that it is the only real world." Auerbach writes:

> The world of the Scripture stories is not satisfied with claiming to be a historically true reality—it insists that it is the only real world, is destined for autocracy. All other scenes, issues, and ordinances have no right to appear independently of it. . . . Far from seeking, like Homer, merely to make us forget our own reality for a few hours, it seeks to overcome our reality: we are to fit our own life into its world, feel ourselves to be elements in its structure of universal history.[12]

Frei, however, adds to Auerbach's literary theory his own analysis of the distinction between meaning and reference in biblical interpretation. The liberal reversal that subjugates the Bible to extrabiblical thought stems from liberalism's confusion of the literal, realistic *meaning* of the biblical narratives with their *reference* to actual, historical events. The Bible's meaning stems from the internal literary world pictured in its stories, not from the external historical world referred to by these stories. That the Bible is not scientifically historical, however, does not entail that it is not historylike; as historylike, the Bible is "literally," though not "historically," true. The Bible is historylike because it weaves together characters and incidents into realistic narrative accounts of reality. But once historical criticism debunked the precritical idea that the Bible ostensively refers to objective history, biblical critics and theologians (according to Frei) proceeded to ignore Scripture's historylike character. Consequently, the narrative genre of the Bible was downplayed even though the recognition of this genre was indispensable for grasping the meaning of the great sagas and stories of Scripture. "A realistic or history-like (though not necessarily historical) element is a feature, as obvious as it is important, of many of the biblical narratives that went into the making of Christian belief. . . . But this specifically realistic characteristic, though acknowledged by all hands to be there, finally came to be ignored."[13]

---

[11]Frei, *Eclipse of Biblical Narrative*, 130.

[12]Erich Auerbach, *Mimesis: The Representation of Reality in Western Literature* (Princeton: Princeton University Press, 1953) 14-15.

[13]Frei, *Eclipse of Biblical Narrative*, 10.

In *The Identity of Jesus Christ,* Frei's constructive proposal is to separate what modern theology and criticism confused—historylikeness and historical facts—and argue for a hermeneutical recovery of the narrated identity of the synoptic Jesus.

Frei's Christology is built on a reading of the Gospel accounts that brackets the historical-critical question as to whether the New Testament reports objective history in order to focus on the character of Jesus as a function of the stories themselves. The Gospels are more like historical novels than scientific treatises; their meaning inheres in what they say literarily rather than in what they refer to objectively. "[The Gospels] are history-like precisely because like history-writing and the traditional novel and unlike myths and allegories they literally mean what they say. There is no gap between the representation and what is represented by it."[14] Frei's confidence that no "gap" exists between the representations of the Gospels' protagonist and the actual identity of Jesus Christ underscores how his theology fulfills the aim of what Lindbeck calls intratextual theology: a redescription of reality (in this case, the reality of Jesus) within the scriptural framework rather than a translation of this reality into extrabiblical categories. Theology, then, is circumscribed within the horizon of the biblical world. Like Lindbeck's grammatical method, Frei envisions theology as a discipline governed by a careful reading of the determinative "patterns" of Jesus' narrated identity in the Gospels.[15]

Scriptural stories and the ecclesial doctrines that stem from them provide the "rules" (Lindbeck) or "patterns" (Frei) for theological reflection. In essence, the Yale school attempts to reverse the "reversal" that absorbed the biblical world into external realities. In addition, the Yale theologians call for a return to the inner-Christian demand of according primacy to the Bible's ruled vision of reality for Christian theology. Communities of integrity that preserve their own intratextual interpretations will find, paradoxically, that their particular experiences are more available to the wider culture than liberalism's best homogenizing attempts at translation. "Religious communities are likely to be practically relevant in the long run to the degree that they do not first ask what is either practical or relevant, but instead concentrate on their own intratextual outlooks and forms of life."[16]

Holmer's *The Grammar of Faith* is another example of the theological family resemblances within the Yale school. Although Holmer does not speak extensively about the precise relationship of Scripture to theology, he does note that the Bible should be understood on its own, intratextual

---

[14]Frei, *Identity of Jesus Christ,* xiv.

[15]Ibid., chap. 14.

[16]Lindbeck, *Nature of Doctrine,* 128.

terms and respected for a vision of reality "completely different" from our own: "Even the Bible can probably be 'understood' (in a certain manner of speaking) not by extending its language into other media, but by using it on one's own behalf to make very clear to oneself how completely different it is, just as it stands. Instead of assuming that there are thoughts, deep and rich, for which the Biblical text is but an approximate and local expression, and which the theologian is qualified to unearth, let us really give honor to the text once more!"[17] Theology should not first translate its subject matter "into other media" because the biblical world is not an "appropriate and local expression" of our best "thoughts, deep and rich." Certainly theology hopes that its interpretation of reality will have an impact on the wider culture, but "honor to the text" preempts translation of the scriptural witness into voguish thought patterns for the sake of theology's conversation with the world. "Of course, we have already said that theology is interpretation; but that does not mean that it is an arbitrary and casual refashioning of a subject matter to suit a whimsical and passing enthusiasm."[18] The problem with modern theology is that it has neglected its fidelity to the biblical world in favor of articulating the relevant meanings of the Christian witness to contemporary culture. Holmer inveighs against those modern cultured despisers who "cannot believe in gods, sins, God, or the devil, but they still need the 'meanings' with which those were linked. So now the theological task, enough to make every Saul into a Paul all over again, is to isolate those meanings and somehow launch them into the sea of humankind!"[19] There can be no question that Paul Holmer shares the agenda of intratextual hermeneutics with both Lindbeck and Frei.

The other point of similarity between Holmer and his Yale colleagues is his definition of theology as the "grammar of Christian faith." We have seen how Lindbeck develops his grammatical theology. Holmer also appropriates Wittgenstein and anticipates Lindbeck's rule theory of doctrine by arguing that Christianity has a corelike "grammar" that governs the structure and organization of the church's "language games." (By "grammar," Holmer simply means "that set of rules that describes how people speak who are doing it well."[20]) According to Holmer, theology is descriptive of the already given, intrabiblical rules that guide the church's appropriation of its rich scriptural and doctrinal heritage. These rules are contained within the master concepts—such as God, Christ, and Church—located in the biblical stories. Theology attends to these rules as gram-

---

[17]Holmer, *Grammar of Faith*, 47.

[18]Ibid., 23.

[19]Ibid., 171.

[20]Ibid., 20.

marlike criteria for correctly speaking about God and the world and must guard against substituting other criteria for these. "[Theology] does not substitute new concepts for those in the [biblical] story, for that again is not improvement but is invariably a radically different replacement. One might say that a new concept usually changes the entire grammar. *Theology is a name, then, for the ruled way, the correct way, of speaking about and worshipping God*"[21][emphasis mine].

Holmer's theological vision is congruent with Lindbeck's notion of doctrines as *regulae fidei* and consistent with Frei's and Lindbeck's intertextual hermeneutics in its recognition of the primacy of the Bible's storied realities for doing theology. And his polemic against contemporary theology's "whimsical enthusiasm" for translating Scripture into its modern "meanings" reverberates the Yale school's attitude toward liberalism. As Holmer trenchantly puts it: "Continuous redoing of the Scripture to fit the age is only a sophisticated and probably invisible bondage to the age rather than the desire to win the age for God."[22]

A third common characteristic of the Yale school is the rejection of theological liberalism's (alleged) commitment to the foundational enterprise of validating traditional theological claims by appeals to philosophical criteria of truth and rationality.[23] The Yale school maintains that there can be no extrabiblical foundations, no ontological grounding, that can prove either the truth or falsity of the Christian witness. In effect, the Yale school's antifoundationalism is a function of its intratextual hermeneutics. If the goal of intratextual theology is to redescribe reality in the language of the Bible and not in extrascriptural categories, then apologetic and liberal approaches to dialogue with Christianity's cultured despisers that seek to ground the scriptural witness by appeals to universal standards of rationality will be avoided as compromising the particular and distinctive message of the Bible.

Yet if theology is antifoundationalist, what is the relationship between it and the other disciplines? If liberal theology errs by grounding the Christian witness on common structures of experience and rationality, is the church's classic apologetic task of offering reasons for its hope in the Gospel thoroughly misplaced? This is not the case, because the

---

[21]Ibid., 203.

[22]Ibid., 23.

[23]I examine the Yale school's twofold understanding of the term *foundationalism* in the second section. For the current philosophical discussion of foundational disciplines that "ground" morals, politics, and religions on "philosophical bases," see Richard Rorty, "Pragmatism, Relativism, and Irrationalism" in *Consequences of Pragmatism* (Minneapolis: University of Minnesota Press, 1982) 160-75. Also see Richard J. Bernstein, *Beyond Objectivism and Relativism* (Philadelphia: University of Pennsylvania Press, 1983).

apologetic task and the conversation with the other disciplines is not wholly scuttled by the Yale theologians. On the contrary, apologetics and interdisciplinary dialogue is carefully maintained, but in a fashion that is now ad hoc and occasional instead of systematic and determinative. Indeed, the call for a nonfoundational "ad hoc apologetics" has become a watchword for the New Yale Theology, and in my opinion, reflects a judicious and balanced model for the relationship between theology and extratheological frameworks. So Lindbeck: "A postliberal approach need not exclude an *ad hoc apologetics*, but only one that is systematically prior and controlling in the fashion of . . . liberalism."[24] And Frei: "I am convinced that the passionate and systematic preoccupation with the *apologetic task* . . . is self-defeating—except as an *ad hoc* and highly various exercise"[25] [emphases mine].

Ad hoc apologetics is predicated on the theologian's prior commitment to the integrity of the Christian tradition and the exigency to explain the faith through the cautious use of extratheological language. This model for apologetics is a variation on Anselm's historic epigram "faith seeking understanding": faith itself demands rigorous thought in order to explicate better its distinctive content. Insofar as theology is like a rule-governed natural language, reason is dependent on the grammatical context in which the language of faith operates. Hence the Yale school's preference for Wittgenstein: reason's role is to uncover the way in which the language-games of the Christian church are played in particular situations. In this scheme critical reflection in the service of theology labors to discern the grammar of Christian faith and does not function as a means for providing noncontextual foundations for faith. Appeals to general standards of reason cannot ground theological claims, but once these claims are made, such standards can advance the intelligibility of these claims. "[T]he logic of coming to believe, because it is like that of learning a language, has little room for argument, but once one has learned to speak the language of faith, argument becomes possible."[26]

To facilitate the credible expression of Christian thought, ad hoc apologetics borrows from other disciplines concepts and expressions for articulating the unique witness of the church. In the case of the Yale theologians, we have seen how Lindbeck and Holmer utilize Wittgenstein, just as Frei borrows from the thought of Erich Auerbach. As Frei

---

[24]Lindbeck, *Nature of Doctrine*, 131.

[25]Frei, *Identity of Jesus Christ*, xii. For a similar understanding, see William Werpehowski, "Ad Hoc Apologetics," *Journal of Religion* 66 (1986): 282-301; and David F. Ford, " 'The Best Apologetics Is a Good Systematics': A Proposal about the Place of Narrative in Christian Systematic Theology," *Anglican Theological Review* 67 (1985): 232-53.

[26]Lindbeck, *Nature of Doctrine*, 132.

comments with reference to Karl Barth, this borrowing effort is legitimate because *"ad hoc* apologetics, in order to throw into relief particular features of [the biblical] world," can formally, though not materially, employ "any and all technical philosophical concepts and conceptual schemes" to explicate the Christian subject matter.[27] This process of borrowing, then, is thoroughly specific to the concrete situations in which Christian witness needs intelligible and defensible explanation; in turn, it seeks to avoid the temptation to allow the other disciplines to control materially, rather than aid formally, the exposition of theology's subject matter. Understandably, this temptation is difficult to avoid, and the Yale school has been quick to point out how extratheological conceptualities have often functioned as Trojan horses in the camp of the church, undermining Christian theology with thought and language foreign to its essence. The culprit in this matter is consistently identified by the Yale school as liberal theology, a charge to which I will direct my attention in the following section.

• Ricoeur and Liberal Foundationalism •

We have seen that the Yale school regards its liberal theological predecessors and contemporaries to be foundationalist in their apologetic concerns. On this issue there is committed agreement. Holmer attacks "theism" as "the kind of theology which still has to *ground* everyday religious language and practice in something [for example, 'being'] that only philosophical concepts can possibly reach."[28] Holmer mentions process theologians Rahner, Tillich, and Heidegger as foundationalist "theists." Frei criticizes "mediating theologians" whose apologetics uncover "a common *ground* between analysis of human experience by direct natural and by some distinctly Christian thought" and thereby "fit the biblical story into another world."[29] He regards such disparate thinkers as John Locke, Schleiermacher, Ritschl, Ebeling, Pannenberg, Rahner, and Moltmann to be united in this apologetic, extratextual task. Lindbeck makes the same point: "This same [apologetic] concern accounts for the liberal commitment to the foundational enterprise of uncovering universal principles and structures—if not metaphysical, then existential, phenomenological, or hermeneutical."[30] And as I have noted, his stronger judgment is that this apologetic interest of modern theology has been "systematically prior and *controlling* in the fashion of post-Cartesian natural theol-

---

[27]Frei, "An Afterword," 114.

[28]Holmer, *Grammar of Faith*, 169.

[29]Frei, *Eclipse of Biblical Narrative*, 129-30.

[30]Lindbeck, *Nature of Doctrine*, 129.

ogy and of later liberalism"[31] [above emphases are mine]. Lindbeck's lineup of liberal foundationalists includes many of the same names as do his colleagues', and his criticism of liberalism is the same: the mistake of modern theology has been the craving for a philosophical foundation on which to base theological reflection.

The Yale theologians seem to be saying two things here. When they speak of foundationalism in the strong sense, they criticize liberals for "grounding" theological claims on general, philosophical foundations that "control" the Christian subject matter. Yet they also understand foundationalism in a weaker sense as the attempt to display "common ground" or experiential "structures" to which theological claims are correlated in order to be made intelligible to moderns. The Yale school appears to understand foundationalism in two related, but distinct, ways: either as the inflated search for universal and context-invariant standards of rationality, or as the more circumspect task of using relatively general criteria of intelligibility to explicate better what the church means on this particular topic at this particular time. My hunch is that this ambiguity surrounding the exact meaning of the term *foundationalism* is not a deliberate attempt at equivocation, but given the weight the Yale school attaches to this charge it is less than reassuring to sense that its complaint against liberal theology is like a slippery cable that runs throughout its whole argument. As such, it is impossible to grasp with any confidence.

What is even more problematic (and indeed ironic) about the Yale notion of foundationalism is that in its "strong" version it does not apply to most of the theologians under question, and in its "weak" version, while it does apply to these theologians, it also applies with equal force to those practitioners of postliberal theology who devised the label in the first place.

To support the first part of this claim, it will be impossible to survey the whole of modern theology in order to see whether or not it is foundationalist. Instead, I will turn to one of the supposed principal sources of foundationalist theological reflection, Paul Ricoeur, to test whether his thought really is a foundationalist enterprise that philosophically controls the free expression of the Christian witness by placing that witness on a philosophical base. The Yale theologians read Ricoeur's thought as enmeshed in an experiential-expressivist understanding of religion that grounds theology on the all-determining experience of the sovereign "central self."[32] According to this reading, Ricoeur is a "strong" foundationalist who supports his theological hermeneutic by a prior philosophical hermeneutic that makes a general theory about common religious

---

[31]Ibid., 131.

[32]Frei, "The 'Literal Reading' of Biblical Narrative," 45, 50, 56. Lindbeck makes the same point with reference to the "experiential-expressive hermeneutics of Paul Ricoeur" in *Nature of Doctrine*, 136.

experience—the experience of the "central self"—the true referent of the biblical stories.

At first glance this interpretation seems viable because of Ricoeur's liberal use of a variety of methodological tools in his theological hermeneutic. At different stages in his own intellectual odyssey he has freely, some might say eclectically, employed a variety of intellectual frameworks—from psychoanalysis, phenomenology, and structuralism, to analytic philosophy and, as we have seen here, narratology and theories of discourse—in order to shed light on the meaning of the biblical texts. The discussion in chapter 3 about explanation attempted to clarify the precise nature of Ricoeur's theological model on this issue ("while theory *guides* it is the text's subject matter which *governs* the interpretive process") so that at no point, theoretically speaking, has Ricoeur's adoption of extra-biblical tools of analysis been an intentional attempt to ground and fix the specific meaning of the biblical witness by an appeal to general categories in phenomenology or some other thought-scheme. "To explain more is to understand better"[33] is the adage he highlights to defend his balancing act of preserving the autonomy and integrity of certain textual expressions while simultaneously employing various explanatory devices to understand better the force of these expressions. But if Ricoeur does not ground his theological hermeneutic on an incorrigible and general philosophical foundation outside the biblical witness, then what is the basis for his hermeneutic? Does he claim simply to be offering a *reading* of Scripture to which we are asked to comport with if that reading is convincingly faithful to the novel possibilities the Bible sets before us?

With the important proviso that no interpretation of Scripture is ever methodologically innocent of the founding biases and assumptions of the exegete, Ricoeur's answer to this question, in a word, would be yes. The sustaining matrix of this reading is not a general theory about human religiosity (though such theories can be used to elucidate certain features of the biblical world) but an immersion in the play of discourses that make up the biblical viewpoint, an immersion in "the most *originary* expressions of a community of faith, [in] those expressions through which the members of this community have interpreted their experience for the sake of themselves or for others' sake."[34] His hermeneutic, then, is based not on general philosophical propositions, or even on "theological statements, in the sense of metaphysical speculative theology," but rather on the variety of biblical "expressions embedded in such modes of discourse as narratives, prophecies, legislative texts, proverbs and wisdom say-

---

[33]Paul Ricoeur, *Time and Narrative,* trans. Kathleen McLaughlin and David Pellauer, 3 vols. (Chicago: University of Chicago Press, 1984–1988) 2:32.

[34]Paul Ricoeur, "Philosophy and Religious Language," *Journal of Religion* 54 (1974): 73.

ings, hymn, prayers, and liturgical formulas."[35] Ricoeur regards himself as a philosopher who listens for the Word and not as a philosopher, or even a theologian, who takes hermeneutical recourse in extrabiblical concepts—or, as he calls it, ontotheological knowledge—that could ground and thereby exhaust the meaning of the biblical message. "I put theological utterances on the same speculative side as philosophical utterances inasmuch as theology's discourse is not constituted without recourse to concepts borrowed from some speculative philosophy, be it Platonic, Aristotelian, Cartesian, Kantian, Hegelian, or whatever. For the philosopher, to listen to Christian preaching is first of all to let go (*se depouiller*) of every form of ontotheological knowledge."[36]

Ricoeur maintains that his hermeneutical procedure is to "let go" of the always-present temptation to locate Christian reflection on a philosophical base that collapses the distinctive meanings of the realities set forth in Scripture into a general philosophical system that defines the meaning of all Reality as such. Some of Ricoeur's commentators say this model is fine in principle, but the question remains for them as to whether he carries out this theoretical commitment in his exegetical practice. Is Ricoeur's hermeneutical aversion to grand ontotheological schemes consistent with his actual handling of the biblical texts? His critics who are indebted to the New Yale Theology do not think so. Frei contends that Ricoeur's thought evidences the stresses and strains of an "uneasy alliance" between making human religious experience *and* the figures of God and Christ the referent of the New Testament stories.[37] William Placher follows this thought and argues that Ricoeur's use of the parables of Jesus shows that "according to Ricoeur the narratives of the parables—which are the biblical narratives he usually discusses—do not function primarily to tell us who God is or what Christ did. Their subject matter, their referent, is human experience."[38]

---

[35] Ibid.

[36] Paul Ricoeur, "Naming God," *Union Seminary Quarterly Review* 34 (1979): 219.

[37] Frei, "The 'Literal Reading' of Biblical Narrative," 50.

[38] William C. Placher, "Paul Ricoeur and Postliberal Theology: A Conflict of Interpretations?" *Modern Theology* 4 (1988): 43. As does Frei in "The 'Literal Reading' of Biblical Narrative," Placher here suggests that Ricoeur's hermeneutical focus falls consistently on the parables, not the other blocks of narrative material in the Bible, because the parables more easily support Ricoeur's case that human experience is the Bible's subject matter. This is a curious observation because Ricoeur's exegetical career, in addition to his work on the parables, has spanned his earlier attention to the Genesis creation stories in *The Symbolism of Evil* and "Sur l'exégèse de Genèse 1, 1–2, 4a" to his more recent interest in the entire Jesus story in "Le récit interprétatif" and, as we have seen, in his unpublished Sarum lectures "Time and Narrative in the Bible."

Ricoeur's critics do have a point here because he does appear to be inconsistent in sometimes identifying the referent of biblical discourse as God or the Word of God, and sometimes as something else (say, human experience or the Kingdom of God). In his *Semeia* article, for example, he restricts the referent of the biblical world to human experience: "In this sense we must say that the ultimate reference of the parables, proverbs, and eschatological sayings is not the Kingdom of God, but human reality in its wholeness."[39]

But this passage should be read in the context of Ricoeur's other comments. The following statement, in contrast, is representative of his more polysemic definition of the biblical referent: "The first task of hermeneutics is not to give rise to a decision on the part of the reader, but to allow the world of being which is the 'issue' of the biblical texts to unfold . . . the proposition of a world which in the biblical language is called a new world, a new covenant, the kingdom of God, a new birth. These are the realities unfolded before the text, which are certainly for us, but which begin from the text."[40] And there are also examples of Ricoeur's theocentric definition of the Bible's subject matter: "God, who is named by the texts which help open up my desire to listen, is, in a way still to be spoken of, the ultimate referent of these texts."[41]

The problem is that Ricoeur appears to define the biblical world in three different ways: as human reality; as a new world or new covenant; and as God. A balanced reading of his overall hermeneutic will, I think, find the solution to this dilemma in recognizing that the biblical referent is understood perspectivally by Ricoeur on the basis of the different biblical contexts in which this referent is presented. From the "fides quae creditur" angle, this referent is mediated in the constellation of realities spoken of in Scripture in which God is the ultimate term or referent of this constellation; from the "fides qua creditur" angle, this referent is human experience reconfigured on the basis of the God-referent narrated in the biblical witness. Both angles of vision are necessary (hence Ricoeur's objections to a Barthlike personalist interpretation of the creation accounts), so that the object-referent of the Bible (God or the New Being) always proceeds from the Bible in order to redescribe imaginatively the subject-referent of these texts (human experience). My sense concerning the bulk of Ricoeur's work on biblical hermeneutics indicates that he wants to preserve both the subject-side and the object-side of the biblical world, his problematic comment in the *Semeia* article notwithstanding.

"The idea of revelation denies the autonomy of the thinking subject inscribed within the idea of a consciousness completely in control of it-

---

[39]Paul Ricoeur, "Biblical Hermeneutics," *Semeia* 4 (1975): 7.

[40]Ricoeur, "Philosophy and Religious Language," 81.

[41]Ricoeur, "Naming God," 217.

self."[42] Rather than providing an experiential basis for his exegetical practice, Ricoeur accents the demand for self-divestment (*dépouillement*) in the process of listening for the biblical witness.

> Listening to Christian preaching also stands in the order of presuppositions, but in a sense where presupposition is no longer self-founding, the beginning of the self from and by the self, but rather the assumption of an antecedent meaning that has always preceded me. *Listening excludes founding oneself.* . . . It requires giving up (*dessaisissement*) the human self in its will to mastery, sufficiency, and autonomy. The Gospel saying "whoever would save his life will lose it," applies to this giving up.[43]

The similarity between Barth and Ricoeur on this issue—not between Ricoeur and theological liberalism—is striking. Whether it is referred to as "acknowledgment" (Barth) or "listening" (Ricoeur), both thinkers argue that comprehension of the scriptural Word in the moment of revelation entails a departure from the philosophical project of providing a neutral basis for accepting the Christian message in the experience of the independent human subject. In no circumstances (and certainly not in the case of divine revelation) is the interpreter a self-positing subject thoroughly transparent to itself as an autonomous center of control. Barth labels a subject-centered basis for theological reflection "Christian Cartesianism,"[44] and Ricoeur contends that "the idea of revelation" opposes "the claim to a complete transparency of truth and a total autonomy of the thinking subject."[45] Apart from *dépouillement*, the self-knowledge of the Cartesian subject inevitably controls the knowledge of the reality of God outside the subject. The process of comprehending the absolute in our history entails the dispossession of the human subject in the recognition of a reality that has preceded the subject and over which the subject has no control. Understanding of revelation, then, is standing under the free object of the biblical witness.

---

[42]Paul Ricoeur, "Toward a Hermeneutic of the Idea of Revelation," in *Essays on Biblical Interpretation*, ed. Lewis S. Mudge (Philadelphia: Fortress Press, 1980) 97.

[43]Ricoeur, "Naming God," 219. Peter J. Albano observes as well: "The narcissistic *Cogito* of the self-positing subject displaced from its autonomous centre is then open to be given to itself by the Word of the Other in which it is constituted in authentic integrity" (Peter J. Albano, "Toward a Dialectical Apologetic of Hope: The Confrontative Dimension of Paul Ricoeur's Contribution to Fundamental Theology," *Studies in Religion/Sciences Religieuses* 15 [1986]: 86).

[44]Karl Barth, *Church Dogmatics* vol. 1: 1, trans. G. W. Bromiley (Edinburgh: T. and T. Clark, 1975) 214-27.

[45]Ricoeur, "Hermeneutic of Revelation," 95.

The exegete is not his own master; to understand is to place himself under the object which is at stake in the text; thus, Christian hermeneutics must be placed in motion by the Announcement which is at stake (Ricoeur).[46]

Acknowledgment consists in the fact that it merely seeks to be the answer to a "recognition"—at this frontier even the meaning of the word must change—which has come to man from beyond all his own acts or powers, of which he himself is not the subject, but in whose free truth and reality he must be acknowledged if he is to acknowledge its truth and reality (Barth).[47]

The displacement of the self in the experience of listening for the Word of God is a hallmark of Barth's and Ricoeur's theological hermeneutics—and a position that separates their standpoints from other philosophical and theological positions that use the experience of the sovereign self as the basis for a theological interpretation theory. In part, Ricoeur's argument against subject-based hermeneutics has its origins in Heidegger's rift with Husserl on this issue; but, as he also points out, it was actually Barth's theology of the Other that initially informed Ricoeur's move beyond Husserl's theory of the controlling transcendental ego: "It was in fact Karl Barth who first taught me that the subject is not a centralizing master but rather a disciple or auditor of a language larger than itself."[48] Or, as he says in his Freud book with reference to Barth, in the encounter with the Word of God, the subject is challenged by a "call, a kerygma, a word addressed to me. In this sense, I am in accord with the way in which Karl Barth poses the theological problem. The origin of faith lies in the solicitation of man by the object of faith."[49]

Self-divestment in the face of the absolute is constituted by a deferral, a subordination to the object of Christian witness as that object has been

---

[46]Paul Ricoeur, "The Critique of Religion," in *The Philosophy of Paul Ricoeur: An Anthology of His Work,* ed. Charles E. Reagan and David Stewart (Boston: Beacon Press, 1978) 222.

[47]Barth, *Church Dogmatics* 1:1, 208.

[48]See Richard Kearney, "Dialogues with Paul Ricoeur," in *Dialogues with Contemporary Continental Thinkers* (Manchester: Manchester University Press, 1984) 27.

[49]Paul Ricoeur, *Freud and Philosophy: An Essay on Interpretation,* trans. Denis Savage (New Haven: Yale University Press, 1970) 523. By way of Eberhard Jüngel, Ricoeur's indebtedness to Barth concerning an anti-Cartesian foundation for theological hermeneutics based on the Word of God is apparent in his brief correspondence with me: "The death of the metaphysical God is essential to grasping God as the one who addressed himself to me and who therefore can be grasped in the Event of the Word alone. . . . the search for a guarantee, begun with the Cogito, starts the discourse of the death of God. Faith is interrupting the need for a guarantee. . . . But all of this is perhaps very Barthian" (letter to author, 24 September 1984).

given in the first-order language of the biblical texts. Of course, second-order theological reflection on this language in the form of doctrines can help work out the conceptual implications in the biblical witness (and Barth, more so than Ricoeur, performs this task admirably). But the initial and fundamental task of theological hermeneutics is to grasp the meaning of the event of revelation itself; and to do this the interpreter must give priority to those types of biblical discourse that the early communities of witness employed to express their own self-understanding of God's action in history. "This is a hard saying for philosophy to understand," as Ricoeur says, but it is only by means of the fragile traces and signs that the absolute gives of itself that knowledge of revelation is possible at all."[50] Barth's and Ricoeur's theological hermeneutics coalesce on this point: knowledge of the Word of God follows a movement away from the pretension of consciousness to constitute itself because this knowledge proceeds only by means of the language of witness present in the early communities' first-order discourse.

Ricoeur's Anselmian concern to use philosophy to understand (not overwhelm) Christian faith is analogous to the Yale school's borrowing of insights from the other disciplines to explicate Christian faith rationally. In this respect his philosophical eclecticism is little different from the Yale school's ad hoc apologetics. Indeed, is Ricoeur's approach formally any different from Holmer's dependence on Wittgenstein's notion of grammar to form his own grammatical theology, Frei's use of analytic philosophy's "intention-action" model and Auerbach's literary realism for his Christology, or Lindbeck's borrowing from cultural anthropology and Wittgenstein to shape his proposal for a rule-governed, postliberal theology? Is not the Yale school also employing points of contact between the other disciplines and Christian theology? Is it not also utilizing extratheological concepts and language in order to render more intelligible to a secular world the distinctive witness of Christian faith? And if so, how is its mediation of Christ and culture really different from Ricoeur's antifoundationalist and intratextual motto that "listening excludes founding oneself"[51] on any ontotheological foundation whenever one does the work of Christian theology?

---

[50]Ricoeur: "It is, in effect, a fact of finitude that original affirmation cannot appropriate itself in a totally intuitive reflection but that it must take a detour through an interpretation of the contingent signs that the absolute gives of itself in history" ("The Hermeneutics of Testimony," in *Essays in Biblical Interpretation*, 148-49); Barth: "And that means in practice that when we are asked how objective revelation reaches man, we can and must reply that it takes place by means of the divine sign-giving" (*Church Dogmatics* 1:2, 233).

[51]Ricoeur, "Naming God," 219.

• Barth and the Truth Status of Theological Language •

A possible rejoinder by the Yale school to the suggestion that its theology is akin to Ricoeur's on this issue might be that its own enterprise is
still more intratextual than liberal theology's was and is. Lindbeck's argument that the "Bible is to absorb reality" is, in my opinion, the corner-
stone of the Yale intratextual approach. But what is the status of such a
claim, and specifically, how is it related to the church's self-understanding that its intrabiblical life has a purchase on extrabiblical reality? What
is the truth status of theological language according to the Yale school?

Clearly, the Yale theologians, unlike some of their more liberal counterparts, are not threatened by the "scandal of particularity"[52] characteristic of the biblical texts and Christian doctrines (for example, the belief
that Jesus Christ is the Son of God). But what truth claims, if any, do such
faith-specific statements make? Can we ever say that such claims are
statements about the world "out there" beyond the church's "in here"
appropriation of its founding persons and events? Is theological discourse something more than a *witness* that instantiates certain grammatical rules (Lindbeck; Holmer), something more than literary *interpretation*
of biblical stories (Frei)? Does not theology also make *assertions* that refer
extra nos to realities that exist independently of this grammar and these
stories?

The general answer of the Yale school to this question is that the truth
of theological discourse inheres in *how* the discourse is used, not in the
realities to which it *refers*. Theological statements are true not because they
correspond to reality as such, but because they constitute a "form of life"
that coheres with the world of the biblical texts.

Each of the Yale theologians we have considered approaches this issue in related fashion. Frei, for example, argues that to ask the question
concerning the reality-reference of the Gospels obscures the central purpose of the stories, which is to narrate the literary identity of Jesus, not
to refer to actual historical events. In the case of the resurrection accounts, the question is the resurrection's "status *in the story*," which is not
that of "reference to an occurrence but simply the affirmation that Jesus'
self-manifestation is in fact the self-manifestation of God."[53] A theological statement is true not because of a correspondence between words and
things but because the statement coheres with the literary world of Scripture. Holmer and Lindbeck, in a similar vein, contend that theological

---

[52]As might be John Hick, e.g., who questions the viability of the Christian doctrine of Incarnation in light of world religious pluralism. See his "Evil and Incarnation," in Michael Goulder, ed., *Incarnation and Myth: The Debate Continued*
(London: SCM, 1979) 77-84.

[53]Frei, *Eclipse of Biblical Narrative*, 315.

language is true to the degree that it correctly exemplifies the grammatical structures of biblical faith. To ask the nagging question of the realist, "Does the church's grammar correspond to the way things really are?" betrays a context-independent definition of truth foreign to how religious statements actually function. They do not refer to objective reality, but instead render the church's contextual vision of the world internally coherent. For Lindbeck, whether a theological statement is true or not is "only a function of [its] role in constituting a form of life"[54] and is not found in its agreement to an extralinguistic order of things.

As we have seen, Lindbeck and Holmer argue that religious witness and doctrinal claims function like grammatical codes. Like a language, Christian faith does not make statements about reality; rather, it organizes reality in a coherent fashion for members of a particular community. Religions and theologies are like languages. We do not ask whether Greek or French or Swahili is *true*, but how it *works* in enabling a community to structure its experience of the world. Likewise, it is a mistake to evaluate theology—now understood as a kind of language or grammar—in terms of its claims to refer to the true nature of God, self, and world. Lindbeck puts it this way: "Just as grammar by itself affirms nothing either true or false regarding the world in which language is used, but only about language, so *theology and doctrine*, to the extent that they are second-order activities, *assert nothing either true or false about God and his relation to creatures*, but only speak about such assertions [emphasis mine]."[55] In other words, second-order theological language, properly understood, makes no reality-claims. Moreover, Lindbeck goes on to argue that first-order discourse is also alethiologically vacuous unless it is uttered in a grammatical context that is experientially consistent with the claim(s) being made. Lindbeck contends that the "meaning, truth, and falsity of [religious] propositions" cannot be "independent of the subjective disposition of those who utter them."[56] We cannot say "Christ is Lord" or "Jesus is the Son of God" and then "cleave the skull of the infidel."[57]

The immediate problem that confronts the church with this position is that it sets aside believers' ability to make first-order assertions about God and world and second-order clarifications of these assertions in the form of doctrines. Yet by virtue of God's own self-communication to us, has not the church's self-understanding always been that it can and does make ontological truth-claims independent of believers' moral dispositions and level of religious commitment? Without this confidence, the

---

[54]Lindbeck, *Nature of Doctrine*, 65.

[55]Ibid., 69.

[56]Ibid., 66.

[57]Ibid., 644.

church finds itself in a Donatistlike position in which the truth and efficacy of the divine presence in the community is determined by the attitudes and behaviors of the community itself. If, for example, I utter "Jesus is the Son of God" while living out of step with the Christian model (say, in the midst of cleaving an infidel's skull), it does not follow that Jesus' status as God's Son is altered by my infidelity. I may misuse this christological title and distort its meaning by employing it in an unbiblical fashion, but my *misuse* is independent of the *truth* of the claim made, a truth that inheres in the relationship of the Son to the Father—not in my proclivity to live (or not to live) the Christian way of life. Lindbeck, however, maintains that the truth of such statements is only a function of their role in organizing a form of life. Indeed, "different religions and/or philosophies may have *incommensurable notions of truth*" because there is *"no common framework . . .* within which to compare religions"[58] [emphases mine].

I think that Lindbeck has confused notions of truth and reference in theological language with notions of meaning and use. As Wittgenstein rightly pointed out, the use of any proposition (theological or otherwise) is generally elucidated by an appeal to how that proposition is intrasystematically "played" in a particular theological "language-game." However, as he also noted, this explanation of language usage does not completely account for the success of this use because this success, in part, depends on the capacity of some statements to refer appropriately to certain states of affairs.[59] Glossing Wittgenstein on this point, Hilary Putnam argues that the success of language use often depends both on *how* language is employed and *whether* that employment really agrees with particular extralinguistic objects—an agreement that achieves the ends of this language-using program. Meaning understood as "use" and truth understood as "reference" (and not simply as coherent usage, as Lindbeck holds) specifies the two complementary, not contradictory, aspects of how language actually works when it accomplishes certain ends. Putnam makes this point with reference to the phenomenon of turning on a light, where something like the reality of "electricity" must be assumed to exist (extralinguistically) in order for us to explain the successful act of flipping on a light switch.

> Nothing in this ["use" theory] account of "use" says *anything* about a correspondence between words and things, or sentences and states of affairs. But it doesn't follow that such a correspondence doesn't exist. A number of tools have this feature: that the instructions for use of the tool do not mention something that *explains* the successful use of the tool. For example, the in-

[58]Ibid., 49.

[59]See Ludwig Wittgenstein, *Philosophical Investigations*, 3d ed., trans. G. E. M. Anscombe (New York: Macmillan Publishing Co., 1958) 95-145.

structions for turning an electric light on and off—"just flip the switch"—do not mention *electricity*. But the explanation of the success of switch-flipping as a method for getting lights to go on and off certainly does mention electricity.[60]

This is not, however, the understanding of language use among the Yale theologians. Without a "common framework" to adjudicate competing reality-claims, Lindbeck, for instance, is forced to conclude (wrongly, in my opinion) that believers do not make ontological "assertions" about the order of reality, but simply "utterances" that are only intrasystematically coherent with their particular religious vision.[61]

Given this relativist understanding of truth, how is the Yale school's claims that the "Bible is to absorb reality" as the "one and only real world" to be understood?[62] The Yale theologians are clear that it is "the religion instantiated in Scripture which defines being, truth, goodness, and beauty."[63] But how can the Bible "define truth" if notions of truth, definitionally, are relative to different intratextual language-games and thereby "incommensurable"? If we can truthfully affirm that the biblical world is the paradigm for all reality, then the Christian community does perforce make reality-claims about the world beyond the biblical texts—namely, that the world as such is best understood and experienced in light of the biblical view of things. But if this is the case, theological language does more than intend meaning-claims about its internal view of things; rather, it clearly does make cross-cultural, context-independent truth-claims about the world per se (as that which should be construed in the terms dictated to us by Scripture).

If we say that the world outside the biblical texts *should* conform to the biblical world, then we imply that the outside world *can* in fact do this. But if we mean that the external world *can* conform to the Bible's world, then we must assume that our language does, in some sense, *tell us something about the external world as such*, namely, that it is that reality which can be molded and shaped by the biblical view of things. If this is the case (and given the Yale theologians' insistence on this point, I do not see how it cannot be), then we do operate with some sort of realist assumption about the world outside the Bible because we are claiming that it should and can conform to our biblical world. We cannot have it both ways: if intratextual theology only gives us intrasystematic vocabulary and not ontological clues about the nature of things, that is fine, but we should

---

[60]Hilary Putnam, *Meaning and the Moral Sciences* (London: Routledge & Kegan Paul, 1978) 99.

[61]Ibid., 63-69.

[62]See nn. 7 and 9 above.

[63]Lindbeck, *Nature of Doctrine*, 118.

then give up the temptation to make reality-as-such claims about what external states of affairs should and can be able to do. But if, on the other hand, we make the general claim that all reality is a candidate for conformity to the biblical worldview, then we should come clean on what *this* claim means—that our language does have the capacity for telling us what the world outside the Bible is or could be—and admit that we are now smuggling into the argument a realist assumption in spite of our anti-realist starting point.

Herein lies the basic contradiction in the Yale school's radical intra-textualism vis-à-vis its relativist alethiology: if we say that the Bible is to absorb the world, then the Christian community does make truth-claims about reality; and yet if notions of truth are as "incommensurable" as Lindbeck suggests, it is difficult to see what force, if any, such an intra-textual claim would have other than as a private wish, a tribal outlook. If the Bible cannot tell us how things in the world "out there" really are but only about how things "in here" seem within its peculiar language-game, then what sense does it make to privilege its language-game over others and maintain that its view of things should be determinative for us, that it should "absorb the world" as the Yale theologians maintain?

It is difficult to reconcile the Yale school's intrabiblical hermeneutics with its relativist notion of truth. Perhaps part of this difficulty stems from its reading of Karl Barth in support of a stance that is sometimes absolutist ("the religion instantiated in Scripture defines truth") and sometimes relativist ("notions of truth are incommensurable"). Karl Barth is virtually the only contemporary theologian that Frei, Holmer, and Lindbeck mention with common approval. Barth's understanding of theology as sustained commentary on the biblical stories is regarded as a model for the Yale school's postliberal "narrative theology." As Lindbeck puts it: "Karl Barth's exegetical emphasis on narrative has been at second hand a chief source of my notion of intratextuality as an appropriate way of doing theology in a fashion consistent with a cultural-linguistic understanding of religion and a regulative view of doctrine."[64]

At first glance, the Yale school's assuming the Barthian mantle seems plausible. Barth labored to redescribe the loci of Christian theology in language and concepts indebted to the Bible, and avoid what he deemed the liberal enterprise of translating the church's discourse into a philosophical vocabulary inimical to theology's true subject matter—God's self-revelation in Jesus Christ. Dogmatic theology's primary dialogue partners are not found in the nontheological world, but in the self-vindicating message of the biblical texts. "Theology can have no more urgent concern than always remaining true to itself . . . as scriptural theology."[65] There

---

[64]Ibid., 135.

[65]Barth, *Church Dogmatics* 1:1, 285.

is no doubt that Karl Barth's own theological hermeneutic is thoroughly intratextual. What is more questionable is whether Barth's thought can be harnessed in the service of the Yale school's relativist understanding of theological truth-claims. For Barth, theology does more than interpret Jesus' narrated identity (Frei) or organize the church's language in coherent fashion (Holmer, Lindbeck). Essentially, theology seeks to follow after its true object, God's self-disclosure in Christ, and proceed from this original revealed fact in all its inquiries. First- and second-order religious language does make ontological "assertions" and not just intrasystematic "utterances" about reality because (a) reality has been disclosed in the Christ-event and (b) that disclosure makes possible the agreement between our language and God's Word. Christian beliefs and doctrines are true to the degree that they are adequate in disclosing the order of things revealed by God. Graham White makes this point well: "Barth's position clearly involves assuming that theological assertions, if true, are true because there is some sort of objective order that they conform to, independently of our ability to recognize them as true; this sort of position is known as *realism*."[66] From a theological realist perspective, for example, the question of the historical reference of the biblical Jesus cannot be bracketed from theology because the church's Scripture witnesses to something more than a character in a story (*pace* Frei). It witnesses as well to a historical occurrence and the Christ alive now in the community's proclamation. And the truth of Christian discourse is not predicated on our subjective dispositions (*pace* Lindbeck); rather, theological truth is dependent on its reference to a revealed "order of being" to which theology seeks conformity. For Barth, theology has its point of departure in "the very definite order of being which Holy Scripture makes manifest, when in its witness to God's revelation it confronts and relates God and man, divine facts and human attitudes, [which] enforces an order of knowing corresponding to it."[67]

Barth's theological dependence on the biblical world is fundamentally more intratextual than the Yale school's postliberal approach. Barth goes beyond interpreting Scripture intratextually. As a realist, he argues that church language, if it is true, is adequate to a revealed reality that does more than witness to a particular intrasystematic viewpoint. Ironically, the theologian the Yale school considers to be a source for its proposals sets forth a theological realism at odds with Lindbeck's understanding of theology as making only "utterances" and not "assertions" about God,

---

[66]Graham White, "Karl Barth's Theological Realism," *Neue Zeitschrift für systematische Theologie und Religionsphilosophie* 26 (1984): 57. For a philosophical defense of a modified realism indebted to Wittgenstein's thought, see Hilary Putnam, *Meaning and the Moral Sciences* (London: Routledge and Kegan Paul, 1978).

[67]Barth, *Church Dogmatics* 1:2, 5.

self, and world. Barth's realism suggests that the church does have a "common framework" for defining truth in its God-given capacity for standing in a right relationship with the order of being given in the divine disclosure.

From my perspective, the "New Yale Theology" has rightly called the church and academic theology back to its primary source, the Bible. And it has deepened this *ad fontes* approach by reminding the Christian community of the pernicious effects that result from some theologians' undue reliance on extratheological base points. But this call has been weakened by the Yale school's ambiguous criticism of liberal foundationalism, as well as by its refusal to adopt something like the theological realism at work in Barth's hermeneutic—a refusal, finally, that makes the postliberal call that the "Bible is to absorb reality" seem platitudinous at best and impossible at worst.

TOWARD A
THEOLOGICAL HERMENEUTIC
OF THE SECOND NAIVETÉ

Nevertheless, my whole energy of interpreting has been expended in an endeavor to see through and beyond history into the spirit of the Bible, which is the Eternal Spirit.[1]

I would dare to say that the Bible is revealed to the extent to which the new being of which it speaks is itself revealing, for the consideration of the world, of the totality of reality, including there my existence and my history. Said otherwise, revelation, if the expression is to have any meaning, is a mark of the biblical world.[2]

• Retrieving the Idea of Revelation in Hermeneutics •

I would like to begin this final chapter with the claim that a hermeneutic of the second naiveté should be linked to the theological presumption that the Other of Christian witness has revealed and does reveal its own self to us. However fragile and tenuous this realist presumption may be that the biblical texts are truly "about something," without it the hermeneutical process founders on the rocks of discrete word-plays and language-games that have no object which can orient and provide direction to the discipline of posing questions to a body of texts that claim, boldly enough, to give us God in writing. I am aware that for many contemporary thinkers even a critical theological realism is untenable, for in

---

[1]Karl Barth, *The Epistle to the Romans*, trans. Edwyn C. Hoskins from the 6th German ed. (Oxford: Oxford University Press, 1933) 1.

[2]Paul Ricoeur, "Philosophical Hermeneutics and Biblical Hermeneutics," in *Exegesis: Problems of Method and Exercises in Reading (Genesis 22 and Luke 15)*, ed. François Bovon and Gregoire Rouiller, trans. Donald G. Miller (Pittsburgh: Pickwick Press, 1978) 331.

its wake this position has often included an apology for an epistemological foundationalism of incorrigible, self-evident basic beliefs, so that many
theologians would like to see this perspective set aside with the ration-
alism of a Descartes or Leibniz. But must the theological realism that is
being suggested here—a self-corrective and always revisable realism—be
contiguous with the rationalist quest for indubitable foundations for *all*
knowledge, theological or otherwise? Why not a realism that has the status of a wager, a hope, a venture, not a realism that hungers for the per-
fect correspondence between mind and reality, but a realism that risks the
belief that what Ricoeur calls the "extraordinarily fragile testimony of the
Gospel" is an authentic redescription of reality? Why not a realism of the
second naiveté, a realism that operates with the presumption of faith
(which, however, many will find hopelessly innocent of the seemingly
irreconcilable pluralism of postmodern existence), a realism that exercises confidence in the possibility that something or someone is referred
to in the biblical accounts, that the divine life itself is being faithfully attested to by the texts that communities of interpretation have found again
and again to be a source of renewal and transformation?

A theological hermeneutic for our time will be best served when it is
clearly informed by an understanding of how God reveals God's self to
us. Without the kind of connection between hermeneutics and revelation
observable in a Barth or a Ricoeur, a theological interpretation theory runs
the risk of becoming one more ceaseless meandering through the endless
intertextuality of the biblical texts, a meandering that is disappointing,
disillusioning, and ultimately unrewarding, because there is no hope
(however precarious that hope may be) that these texts are finally about
something of ultimate value. One of the primary difficulties with the New
Yale Theology is that in spite of its signature concern for the priority of
the biblical framework in theological interpretation, it has not offered a
coherent defense of the ontological or revelational reference of biblical
language. Moreover, in Frei's claim that key biblical events (like the resurrection) have only a story-bound status and make no reference to actual occurrences, and in Lindbeck's argument that Christian language
makes no first-order truth claims, there becomes apparent an odd and
unnerving affinity between their theological intratextualism and the free-
floating intertextualism of both New Critical and deconstructionist poetics: each of these theories accents the self-enclosed immanence of figurative discourse at the expense of the extralinguistic reality-claims that
are at the heart of great religious classics such as the Bible.

Thus, a particular advantage to reading Barth and Ricoeur together is
that both thinkers, in spite of their many and significant differences, point
the way toward letting the Bible be the Bible—toward a healthy confidence in the capacity of the biblical witness to refigure and mediate a world
to the reader without falling prey to the sirens of naive realism and the
metaphysics of presence. In this way they are able to express a theolog-

ical framework that unites the process of interpretation with the disclosure of the God witnessed to in the texts being interpreted. Ricoeur's
theological hermeneutic operates with the presupposition, always under
suspicion of being a vicious circle, that the divine life itself is referred to
and adequately named through the network of competing discourses that
make up the biblical world. His hermeneutical agenda consistently resists what I have called the "textualist" temptation to deny the text's referential function so that he can see afresh how reality can be remade by
the Bible—to see through and beyond the *what* of biblical discourse (its
sense) to the *about what* of this discourse (its reference). Barth, similarly,
even as early as 1918, took issue with the practitioners of the then-reg-
nant historical-critical method who assigned more weight to the scientific
discipline of historical exegesis than to the always more difficult (but also
more important) task of seeing "through and beyond history into the spirit
of the Bible, which is the Eternal Spirit."[3] Like Ricoeur, he bristled at the
thought that an exegete's methodological constraints could put limits on
what the textually mediated God of the Bible would be "allowed" to say
to us today.

Discussions about revelation have, somewhat surprisingly, returned
to contemporary theology. Recently, a steady stream of books and articles has appeared that attempts to explore the experiential and conceptual foundations of the time-honored Christian conviction that God has
revealed and does reveal God's own self to us. In our time, however, this
conviction is not buoyed by the same theological consensus of a generation ago, which spoke confidently of God as revealing himself in history
through his Word and mighty acts. Today revelation is no longer understood by most theologians primarily in terms of the uniform and gender-
biased disclosure of God himself to Western Christians. Instead, its occurrence is conceived as a highly mysterious and thoroughly mediated
event of surprise in which God, no longer strictly defined as Father or Lord
according to the set formulae of theological orthodoxy, is also now named
as Lover or Liberator or Healer on the basis of the always unexpected dis-
closures of the divine life across the fractured spectrum of our diverse
backgrounds and experiences.

Even this more inclusive and pluralistic notion of revelation is rejected by some contemporary theologians, however. Some are opposed
to any retrieval of the doctrine of revelation at all. They lament the reprise
of this troubled concept, fearing it to be a rearguard reaction by struggling conservatives to shore up the shaky foundations of traditional
Christian belief. In their view, the theological moorings of Protestant neoorthodoxy and Catholic neo-Thomism that supported the idea of revelation have long since rotted away, leaving nothing in their place but a

---

[3]Barth, *Romans*, 1.

dizzying array of various genitive theologies (such as liberation theology or feminist theology). The result is that many avant-garde theologians regard the current interest in revelation to be the terminal gasp of a dying mainstream Christian culture as it struggles to reassert its hegemony in a world splintered by theologies of this or theologies of that.

The spirit of the age, in this view, is uncertain, suspicious, postmodern; it is permeated with a sense of "irrevocable loss and incurable fault . . . by the overwhelming awareness of death—a death that 'begins' with the death of God and 'ends' with the death of our selves."[4] Influenced by Derrida's and Foucault's deconstructionist exposé of the radically troubled and unstable nature of our thought and culture, we have seen how postmodern theologians use deconstruction as the new hermeneutic of the death of God. Under the shadow of the Bomb and with the ever-present memories of Auschwitz and Cambodia, history appears Godless, and the Western person experiences less the triumph of grace proclaimed from the pulpit and more the Nietzschean verdict that God has died and we have killed him. Joyce's haunting observation that human history is a nightmare from which we are struggling to awake seems even more apropos today than it did in 1916. Amidst such despair, I find it remarkable that a few thinkers have suggested that a salvaging of the idea of revelation can provide a way beyond the pessimistic malaise that marks our culture.

The reappraisal that I am proposing here will seek a middle course between the new deconstructionist death-of-God sensibilities and the older certainties of a bygone Western Christian monoculture. In keeping with the older tradition, this middle course considers any contemporary retrieval of the idea of revelation adequate only if it accords a special primacy to the biblical texts as the primary medium for the disclosure of the divine life. By the same token, this reappraisal is linked with the postmodern insight that the great biblical stories that undergirded the older revelation-based theologies are not as uniform and secure in their meaning as was once assumed. In our period the Bible has emerged from being a stable book with a central message to being a complicated text or "intertext" with no reliable center. A revisionary notion of revelation, then, will work on the basis of the dual recognition that this category should, indeed, be the linchpin of a contemporary Christian theology based on the biblical witness, but it will also maintain that this witness is fraught with more ambiguity and multiple meanings than previous theologians and exegetes had thought to be the case. In what follows, I will propose a modest number of thesis statements concerning the prospects for a hermeneutic of the second naiveté that takes account of the retrievals and rejections of the idea of revelation that are taking place in theology today.

---

[4]Mark C. Taylor, *Erring: A Postmodern A/theology* (Chicago: University of Chicago Press, 1984) 6.

1. *If and when revelation has occurred within the Christian environment, this disclosure should be understood as the undeserved and wondrous event of God's grace toward us, not as a predictable occurrence whose theoretical justification is found in a theory about the religious nature of humankind.* Ronald Thiemann argues this thesis in his book *Revelation and Theology: The Gospel as Narrated Promise*, a work that is at the forefront of the current retrieval of the idea of revelation.[5] He maintains that without a clear defense of the basic conviction that God reveals God's self to us, our network of beliefs that are supported by this conviction (that God is gracious, that Jesus reveals God, and so forth) is itself without support. Modern theologians have recognized this structural problem, but instead of returning to the inherently powerful testimonies to divine disclosure in the Bible as the only viable basis for belief in revelation, they have developed justifications for the possibility of God's self-disclosure on the basis of theories about the "universal religious dimension" within human experience. In Karl Rahner's theology, for example, we read that all human beings enjoy a deep and fundamental awareness of God that makes God's disclosure to us plausible and meaningful. We all possess an implicit knowledge of and love for God that allows us, as Rahner puts it, to be "ready hearers" of a possible word of revelation from God.[6] With the exception of Karl Barth and a handful of others, most theologians of the recent past who espoused a doctrine of revelation did so on the basis of a Rahnerlike theory about the primordial unity between God and the human person.

In deference to such theories, many theologians today continue to scuttle sustained appeals to the biblical accounts as our most reliable source for knowledge about revelation. Thiemann argues for a reversal in this standard approach: "A doctrine of revelation ought not to be conceived as an epistemological theory but as an account which justifies a set of Christian convictions concerning God's gracious identity and reality."[7] Philosophically and theologically confident approaches to the problem of revelation grounded on the notion that human beings have an implicit knowledge of God make little sense today. In our age of the "wounded cogito," little—if anything—can be inferred about who we are in our deepest selves. What we know about who we are and who God is is best gleaned from a patient hearing of the biblical message, not through a theological depth-analysis of our supposed unity with God. Revisionary theologians such as Thiemann steer attention away from these earlier anthropological claims and focus instead on the provocative stories about,

---

[5]See Ronald F. Thiemann, *Revelation and Theology: The Gospel as Narrated Promise* (Notre Dame: University of Notre Dame Press, 1985).

[6]See Karl Rahner, *Hearers of the Word*, trans. Michael Richards (New York: Herder and Herder, 1969) esp. 130-80.

[7]Thiemann, *Revelation and Theology*, 7.

and images of, God's self-revealedness in the Bible as our best and most persuasive source for construing who we are and what it means to say that God is revealed to us.

Regarding this issue, I find Barth's hermeneutic to be especially powerful and acutely sensitive to the postmodern insight that the human condition really is characterized by what the Swiss theologian labeled the *krisis*—which, in part, stands for the creaturely fault-lines and limitations that render our supposed prethematic unity with God a chimera. In this scheme, there is no ontological identity between us and God (the "analogy of being" in classic Christian theology). In contrast, say, to Rahner's supernatural existential or Tillich's ultimate concern, Barth maintains that the human person has no prethematic or depth knowledge of God. And though I agree with many of Barth's commentators who deem his radical division between God and the human person to be (at least in some instances) too sharply drawn,[8] his disturbing reading of the human situation seems to me to be very close to what is needed in developing a view of revelation that is both right for our time and true to the biblical heritage. He contends that because the image of God within us has been shattered after the Fall, we have no inherent ability for rightly hearing the Word of God.[9] Against the stream of his own Reformation heritage (against Calvin's position that the image of God is corrupted, not destroyed in the human, and against Brunner's argument that a point of contact between the human and God survives the Fall), Barth maintains that we have no capacity for God, no predisposition toward hearing a possible Word from God, no inherent possibility of any correct knowledge of God, no dynamic eros that quests after God, no *analogia entis* between God and ourselves.

But if God is so radically beyond our experience, how is knowledge of God possible at all? It is *possible*, Barth says, because the *actual* grace of God through the spirit of God has performed a miracle in the human heart by allowing us to hear the Word in the words written and spoken by others. This is the point behind Barth's discussion of Paul's "analogy of faith" in Romans 12:6 in contradistinction to the traditional idea of the *analogia entis*.[10] The possibility of our knowledge of God is not predicated on any "secret likeness" between God and us, but on the faith that the Spirit of God gives to each of us. Knowing and experiencing God is God's gift, not our privilege: we discover God not because God is implicitly known by us in our deepest selves, but because our whole being is known explicitly by God, so

---

[8]Thiemann makes this point in *Revelation and Theology*, 94-96.

[9]Karl Barth, *Church Dogmatics* 1:1, trans. G. W. Bromiley (Edinburgh: T. and T. Clark, 1975) 238-39.

[10]Ibid., 239.

that here we discover a reality nearer to us than we are to ourselves, "the hidden home at the beginning and end of all our journeyings."[11]

It is here as well where I think much of the promise of the New Yale Theology lies. In chapter 4 I suggested that this approach (in spite of its antifoundationalism) is not opposed to the use of standards of context-dependent rationality in theology, but rather to a dependence on (seemingly) neutral, universal criteria to ground theology's discourse intellectually and thereby further communication of the gospel. As Lindbeck puts it: "Anti-foundationalism, however, is not to be equated with irrationalism. The issue is not whether there are universal norms of reasonableness, but whether these can be formulated in some neutral, framework-independent language."[12] So, for example, the Yale theologians argue (in a fashion consistent with Barth and Thiemann) that a Tillich or a Rahner errs in his respective attempt to abstract from the distinctive Christian experience of God a general human directionality toward the divine life that can then be used apologetically in conversation with the world. Certainly, if all men and women possess a prethematic awareness of God, then theology's task of explicating the distinctive nature of the Christian God is more plausible. Yet this process of abstraction and generalization runs the risk of developing a foundational scheme that controls the witness of the biblical texts (a witness that says little, if anything, about a transcendental awareness of God) through presuppositions as to what must be the case in reality as such. For the Yale school, there are no depth-analyses of human ontology or knock-down transcendental arguments that can undergird theology's difficult task—a task that consists of giving reasons for Christian faith on the basis of the inherent appeal of the biblical witness alone.

Of course, the gamble in this Bible-specific approach is great as it holds in abeyance many of the questions that defined the interests of theological modernism: are human beings inherently religious? does revelation come from within or from without? But the gamble is worth it because this new tack allows the biblical witness to God's revelation to exercise again its strange and captivating hold on the hearts and imaginations of people today. And in the grip of the biblical witness, we find that new questions with new answers are posed to us (could God be as radically different from us as the Bible suggests? is the strange world of the Bible a world that I could risk inhabiting?)—questions with answers that do not rely on any built-in knowledge of God that we might possess.

2. *If and when revelation has occurred within the Christian environment, this disclosure should be read through the polyphonic play of meaning within the Bible,*

---

[11]Barth, *Romans*, 46.

[12]George A. Lindbeck, *The Nature of Doctrine: Religion and Theology in a Postliberal Age* (Philadelphia: Westminster Press, 1984) 130.

a play that should not be stopped by an isolation of one trajectory of meaning within Scripture as "the" biblical message. If my first point argued the importance of grounding a retrieval of the idea of revelation on the biblical texts, this point highlights how difficult such a task is. Although neo-Reformation theologians, for example, were correct in assigning a central role to the doctrine of revelation in their Bible-centered theologies, they nevertheless did so with little recognition of the diversity and plurality within the biblical texts they cited in support of their positions. Their problem lay in their unawareness of the complicated textuality of the Bible—its crisscrossing referents and indeterminate language, its multiple layers of meaning and open-ended story-lines (as Ricoeur compellingly demonstrates in his narratological reading of Mark), all of which frustrate our attempts to make some final judgment concerning what the biblical witness to revelation is all about.

In the neoorthodox framework the Bible is read as a more or less stable book with a clear and central message. The result is that many of its basic images for God—images that are often male-biased, anthropocentric, and martial in tone—are lifted up as essential to "biblical revelation" or the "biblical view of things." Hence, the great diversity of discourses about and images for the divine reality in Scripture go unnoticed. What is not seen is the always unnerving and yet liberating potential of the Bible to rewrite the accepted script for what constitutes "biblical revelation" by its interweaving, intertextual, open, and diffuse play of meaning. Joseph S. O'Leary, another contemporary theologian interested in linking hermeneutics and revelation, accents this theme: "If we take seriously the materiality of the traditional texts we find that the pure 'word' they wish to communicate is constantly reinvolved in the opacity of the play of signifiers and the play between texts ('intertextuality')."[13]

Here the important disagreements between Barth and Ricoeur come to the fore. As we have observed, does the biblical world display an anthropological bias in which revelation operates primarily on a God-human axis, as Barth says? Or are not the biblical texts better understood as situating anthropological issues within a broader, more global context as only one of many concerns, as Ricoeur suggests? Related to this issue is the question whether (with Barth) we read the Bible with a "christological concentration" or whether we believe (with Ricoeur) that theology and exegesis operate with a plurality of reference points, none of which can be resolved into a single Christ-centered focus.

Ricoeur's interdisciplinary attention to issues in genre analysis and narrative theory permits a consistent openness in his hermeneutic to the polyphony in the biblical text-world that is sometimes (though not al-

---

[13]Joseph S. O'Leary, *Questioning Back: The Overcoming of Metaphysics in Christian Tradition* (Minneapolis: Winston Press, 1985) 41.

ways) lacking in Barth's. Old and New Testament are a *fête du sens:* an ensemble of interdependent voices animated by an interest in projecting a world of unimagined possibilities for the reader. The biblical world is both open in the plurality of readings it can sustain and centered by the role of its God- and Christ-referents, which help to coordinate the Bible's many voices. Yet these organizing referents do not create a homophonic world in which all of Scripture has only one meaning, a christocentric meaning. Barth always upheld the possibility of many readings in interpreting Scripture, but Scripture has only one voice for Barth: the voice of Jesus Christ, the voice that was barely audible in the Hebrew Scriptures and now in the New Testament is so clear that it controls all of the Bible's other manners of speaking. A theological hermeneutic for today will profit by attending to Ricoeur's close reading of the Bible's multifaceted world, a reading that offers a corrective to Barth's argument that all of Scripture should be pressed into the service of a christocentric interpretation.

A hermeneutic of the second naiveté will focus on the give-and-take between text and audience; it will maintain that Scripture is more like a lively and open-ended game between its world and the world of the reader than it is a closed book whose meaning is exhausted by the standard theological lexicon. "[I]t is only through the interplay of text and present situation, in the context of the effective-history of the text, that the meaning of the biblical witness emerges."[14] In this to-and-fro movement between text and reader, God, at one moment, is the Mighty Warrior who goes to battle and the Lord who crushes his enemies. Yet this martial and patriarchal imagery is questionable in a time when many of us have been victimized by sacralized violence. Fortunately, the biblical God is also pictured in Scripture as the Wisdom who laughs at human folly; the Mother who broods over her young; the Fountain whose living water brings eternal life for those who drink from it; the Liberator of the poor, the captive, the disabled, and all those who are downtrodden; and as the Friend of all of us who walk the road to Emmaus after the dark nights of our own souls. The approach I am recommending finds a new flexibility in its hermeneutic, a new suppleness in its understanding of what it means to say and experience that God reveals God's self to us. Seeing God again in the often strange and always multifaceted world of the Bible, theologians retrieving the idea of revelation today are reminding us that the different modalities of the divine life within the biblical texts can free us all to live creatively and expansively in a world whose capacity for change has gone flat and whose vision for the future has become narrow and short-sighted.

Three possible ways open before us today as we consider the possibility of retrieving the doctrine of revelation. We can go back to previous

---

[14]David J. Bryant, *Faith and the Play of the Imagination* (Macon GA: Mercer University Press, 1989) 168.

neoorthodox and neo-Thomist formulations of it, but in each instance we discover the promise and the problems noted above. Both theological schools rightly accorded pride of place to the category of revelation, but the former did so without acknowledging the Bible's polysemy and literary variety, while the latter did so on the foundation of the highly questionable assumption that we possess an innate openness and love for God that serves as the condition for the possibility of God's self-disclosure to us. The way forward is not the way backward, but where does that leave us?

We have yet a second option, which is to scrap altogether any attempt to recover the idea of revelation as doomed from the start. The present-day call is for theology to throw off the heavy shackles of tradition, to resist the temptation to re-employ shop-worn phrases such as *revelation* or the *Word of God*, since they betray a Bible-specific network of questions and answers that is no longer viable. Today we are enjoined to celebrate with the new Nietzschean theologians of deconstruction the death of God and the end of theology. Given that we are precariously alive in a nuclear world at a time when God appears to have been eclipsed by the principalities and powers of the age, should not our most authentic position be that of joining hands with these honest critics of Christian belief who are learning to dance the "dance of death upon the tomb of God"?[15] With the breakdown of the previous theological consensus, and in the face of unprecedented global suffering and crisis, is not deconstruction the best and only response we can make with a sense of integrity?

At first glance the answer might seem to be yes—this attitude of suspicion and defiance seems best suited to the spirit of our time. Yet, the tradeoff in adopting this stance is too costly, because in dancing only to the new music of deconstruction we run the risk of becoming deaf to God's revelatory Word as that Word is mediated through the words of the biblical witness. Is it impossible that God has spoken and could again speak to us today through Scripture? And if it is not, should we not gather together in communities of hope and resistance to hear and understand better what it is God might be saying to us in our time?

If a hermeneutic of the second naiveté is to be viable, then it must be brought together with a rehabilitation of the doctrine of revelation, a revival of the historic expectation Christians have always had toward the possibility that God might speak to us a Word in our history. Granted, such a Word will never have the same monolithic uniformity for us (and thankfully so) that it had for previous generations because we have become acutely aware of how insinuated that Word is in the crisscrossing complexity of the biblical words, of how interdependent that Word is in

---

[15]Carl A. Raschke, "The Deconstruction of God," in *Deconstruction and Theology*, ed. Thomas J. J. Altizer et al. (New York: Crossroad Press, 1982) 27.

the conflict of images of God within Scripture. We have also become aware of our situation-specific location in structures of history, class, and gender. Thus, we can see afresh the Bible's creative diversity as we struggle to build new human communities inspired by the biblical message. Revived interest in the doctrine of revelation can help facilitate this task in a world worn down by pessimism and despair.

3. *If and when revelation has occurred within the Christian environment, this disclosure should set free a mature naiveté toward the world projected by the biblical texts—a strange and potentially subversive world that refigures and enlarges our everyday worlds by asking each of us to risk inhabiting its imaginative space.* What exactly is this strange world of the biblical witness? The answer is that it is neither a direct and unmediated description of past facts, nor a purely imaginary and self-enclosed construction by its authors. It is rather a highly imaginative attempt to configure past, historical events into a meaningful, storied whole. It is narrative fiction with a historical interest or, to put it another way, it is a historically mediated remembrance of a series of events that is animated by the literary imaginations of its creators. While this world bears all the earmarks of literary art through its utilization of character and story line, its use of artistic license is modulated by its theological intent to depict faithfully the actual events that make up the content of its witness. Such a claim concerning the "fictive" dimensions of the biblical texts may prove untenable for some believers who long for Baconian certainty in their investigation of the historicity of the biblical texts; and, as Barth says, the positivist "historian may find this disconcerting and suspicious (or even provocatively interesting)."[16] Both believer and historian, therefore, may find this difficult, but how can a hermeneutic of a second naiveté be otherwise—a hermeneutic that recognizes that all discourse about God, including that of the Bible, both is and is not adequate to that about which it speaks. While this interpretation theory seeks a mature openness to the Bible, it cannot be a hermeneutic of first innocence in which the biblical language is hallowed as a nonmediated and exact copy of the divine will and message.

At the intersection, then, between history and fiction, this hermeneutic will deploy a nonhistoricist concentration on the play of subject matters unfolded by the biblical texts. The focus will not be on the authorial intentions or sociohistorical contexts of the biblical writers, but on the ensemble of God- and Christ-references that burst the boundaries of our everyday worlds by challenging us to new visions of reality. De-emphasis on the world behind the biblical texts is the negative condition for a hermeneutical openness toward the transformative witness of the biblical message in front of the texts. Barth's focus on the texts' *Sache* and Ricoeur's attention to the "about something" of the Bible are apparent in

---

[16]Barth, *Church Dogmatics* 4:1, 320.

their respective models of interpretation: the Bible as Scripture is accessible to us today not on the basis of a reconstruction of its historical origins or authorial intentions, but in light of a literary-theological construal of the compelling vision to which it bears witness. Scripture's *Sitz im Wort*, therefore, is emphasized over its *Sitz im Leben* or *Sitz im Autor*.

Assigning priority to the text's subject matter in interpretation is a rule that applies to all general hermeneutics. A contemporary theological hermeneutic would benefit from Barth's and Ricoeur's formulations of the dialectic between general and special hermeneutics: as the interpretation of the meaning of written discourse, theological hermeneutics is a species of general interpretation theory, but by virtue of its special subject matter, the Word of God, it is a unique form of inquiry with a particular set of problems peculiar to this subject matter. While Barth and Ricoeur both agree that theological and biblical hermeneutics are regional disciplines that apply philosophical categories and tools to the interpretation of Christian texts, they also reverse this order and subordinate general (or philosophical) hermeneutics as a regional *organon* of theological and biblical hermeneutics. Centered on the notion of the text, a contemporary theological hermeneutic would look to interpret the biblical Word as a word like any other human word and as a message of supreme importance, with interpretation theories from other disciplines alternately operating as both the paradigm for, and as the *organon* or instrument of, theological hermeneutics.

Like the Yale theologians' nonfoundationalist ad hoc apologetic, the hermeneutic proposed here will be vigilant against any easy alliances with extrabiblical frameworks of meaning and truth. It will welcome the demise of all ontotheological and metaphysical projects that seek to ground theology on the basis of a general philosophical system. It will claim that it is not possible to translate the language and images of Christian discourse into nonfigurative and single-meaning terms that are conceptually more rigorous and more exact than the church's story-bound, first-order witness to the Word of God. "The death of the metaphysical God," Ricoeur writes, "is essential to grasping God as the one who addresses himself to me and who therefore can be grasped in the Event of the Word alone."[17] Theology is not a straightforward variation on philosophical discourse with terms such as *God* or *Word* being easily redefinable as concepts such as 'being' or 'truth' without any loss of meaning. "The word 'God' does not function as a philosophical concept, whether this be being either in the medieval or the Heideggerian sense of being . . . the word 'God' says more: it presupposes the total context constituted [by the

---

[17]Paul Ricoeur, Letter to author, 24 September 1984.

Bible]."[18] Whenever theology is hermeneutically sensitive to the surplus of meaning always present in the Bible's competing modes of discourse, it will remain suspicious of any philosophical and conceptual terminology that offers one-to-one equivalents to Scripture's diverse ways of speaking.

A mature hermeneutic will resist the allure of all philosophical systems—including those antiphilosophies, such as deconstruction, that reject the biblical texts' reality attestations as referential illusions. By the same token, it will also recognize that the road back to the "precritical" or "scientific" biblicism of a first naiveté is no longer available to us either. Biblicism is always, finally, historicism, whether it is under the guise of the fundamentalist attempt to recover the Bible's *brutum factum*, or whether it appears as the neoliberal quest for the *ipsissima verba* of the so-called historical Jesus. To enclose the biblical literature within a world of its own (be it the historicist world behind the Bible or the textualist world within it) is to turn a deaf ear to the dangerous ontology at work in its struggle to relocate us in the universe of its own distinctive discourse by dislocating our received paradigms for what can and cannot count as reality. In an age that is understandably wary and weary of theological and ecclesiastical authoritarianism, the point must still be made that the Bible does speak with passionate authority about the trustworthiness of its message. But this authority, as Barth says, "has nothing in common with tyranny, because its true likeness is not the power of natural catastrophe which annihilates all human response, but rather the power of an appeal, command and blessing which not only recognizes human response but creates it."[19] This is not the language of revelational positivism, of theological violence to our this-worldly situation that Barth is often accused of[20]; instead, this is an entreaty to all of us who have traveled to the end of the hermeneutical arc, to the moment of appropriation, to risk allowing the Bible to speak to us again in the power of its appeal to our hearts and imaginations.

Ricoeur often speaks of the correlation between seeing-as and being-as as the key to personal appropriation. When the reader ventures *seeing* the environment around her *as* the biblical world portrays it, she discovers this environment to *be as* something provocatively different from what

---

[18]Paul Ricoeur, "Philosophy and Religious Language," *Journal of Religion* 54 (1974): 83. Barth makes a similar point in his disagreement with Kant, with reference to Kant's claim that the term *God* can be construed analogously to the rational idea of an unlimited being. See *Church Dogmatics* 2:1, 179-204.

[19]Barth, *Church Dogmatics* 1:2, 661.

[20]So Heinz Zahrnt's Bonhoefferian interpretation of Barth's project in *The Question of God*, trans. R. A. Wilson (New York: Harcourt Brace Jovanovich, 1969) 85-132.

she had originally thought it to be. The text adumbrates what is by enticing us to see things as the text projects they might be. Reality actually can be remade and augmented by the increase in being that the text displays in front of itself. In this way, the text's ontological surplus fundamentally challenges our post-Enlightenment habits of relying on technical, nonfigurative language to describe everything, a habit of mind and heart that has left most of our experiences thin and brittle and devoid of a discourse by which they can be made meaningful. Today, our individual and everyday worlds remain underdeveloped and impoverished because we no longer have a public language that speaks to the dimensions of ultimacy in the world. The pathos of our time is that we no longer have a common spiritual discourse, a common mythos, for the interpretation of the manifold of experience.[21] The response to this problem by the thinkers we have considered here is, Let the text speak for itself, and see whether the imaginative depictions of reality it unfolds are not fanciful dreams but, rather, ontologically rich and full projections of another way of being in the world, another form of life for ourselves and the earth, that liberates what is essential to us by suggesting what is possible for us. Through Scripture's figurative variations on reality, the imagination is appealed to so that we might see the world as the text depicts it, and the will is empowered to actualize the possible ways of being in the world that the text projects.

This, we have seen, is the true telos of a theological hermeneutic of the second naiveté, what Ricoeur calls "putting the Word to work"[22]: to allow the texts that I have loved and interpreted to be a poetics of my liberation in a concern for others, in solidarity with the planet, and in discipleship to the God of the biblical message. What this interpretive task offers is the remarkable possibility of a second hermeneutical innocence

---

[21]Whether the language and images of the biblical traditions can again meet this need is an open question. But a number of recent proposals specific to this demand in the American context can be cited. Charles Mabee's *Reimagining America: A Theological Critique of the American Mythos and Biblical Hermeneutics* (Macon GA: Mercer University Press, 1985) suggests that an explicitly public and interdisciplinary reading of the Bible—a reading that retypologizes the American mythos in the light of the rich imagery of the Bible—can satisfy our quest for meaning by locating us in a master narrative that has proven in the past to be constructively transformative of our collective experience. I also think Lindbeck's *Nature of Doctrine* and David Tracy's *Plurality and Ambiguity: Hermeneutics, Religion, Hope* (New York: Harper & Row, 1987) offer similar proposals, but in ways that are strikingly different and therefore illustrative of the problem we all face: the articulation of a vocabulary of common myths and symbols by which the human project can be interpreted and rendered meaningful again.

[22]Paul Ricoeur, "Naming God," *Union Seminary Quarterly Review* 34 (1979): 226.

to the claims of Scripture; the hope that the mystery of the Bible can be construed as speaking again to the cultured despisers among us; indeed, the expectation, as Ricoeur says, that "by *interpreting* we can *hear* again."[23]

---

[23]Paul Ricoeur, *The Symbolism of Evil*, trans. Emerson Buchanan (Boston: Beacon Press, 1967).

· INDEX ·

ad hoc apologetics, 62-63, 89, 103, 122
allegory. *See* trope, tropology; typology
analogia entis, 116
Anselm, 95, 103
anthropocentrism, ix, xiv, 71-78, 118
appropriation (application), 52, 56-57,
  68-71, 123
Auerbach, Erich, 91, 95, 103
Augustine, 18, 62, 65-66
authorial intention, 11-12, 21, 33-35, 56,
  65, 121
authority, 5, 123
autonomy, semantic, 13, 33-34, 44

Barth, Karl, vii-xv, 41-42, 100-103, 108-
  110, 115
  and God, 6, 53
  and hermeneutics, 1-26, 51-85, 116-25
  and historical criticism, 6-13, 60
  and Jesus Christ, 15-26, 68-69, 78-85,
  118
  and revelation, 10, 60, 101, 108-10,
  111
  and the Word, 1-9, 12, 19, 24-26, 62,
  68
Berkouwer, G. C., 3, 80
betrayal, 45-46
Bible, interpretation of. *See* Barth and
  hermeneutics; hermeneutics; Ricoeur and hermeneutics
biblicism, 7-8, 123

Bultmann, Rudolf, xiii, 2, 3, 53-55, 57-
  60, 61-62, 68, 71, 82
Calvin, John, 25, 61
Cartesianism, 29, 99, 101, 102
Christ-event. *See* Barth and Jesus Christ;
  Ricoeur and Jesus Christ
christocentrism, ix, xiv, 78-85
christology. *See* Jesus Christ
Church Dogmatics, xi, 3, 10, 16, 52, 83-85
classic, 4, 112
content/form. *See* form/content
cosmology, ix, 37-40, 58-59. *See also*
  ecology
death of God, viii, xii, 23, 102, 114, 120
deconstruction, viii, 13, 18-20, 26, 44-45,
  51, 112, 114, 116, 120, 123
Derrida, Jacques, xiv, 18-20, 23, 114
demythologization, xv, 54-55, 58-59, 71
dépouillement, xiv, 101
dialectical method, 10
différance, 19, 24
discourse analysis, xiii, 11, 13, 27, 30-40,
  57-59, 67, 82-85, 98, 103
ecology, 38-40, 72-78
election, 16
Eliade, Mircea, 37-38
Enlightenment, the, viii, xii, 14, 25, 29,
  90, 124
evil. *See* theodicy
exegesis. *See* Barth and hermeneutics;
  hermeneutics; Ricoeur and hermeneutics

existentialism, 3, 54, 59, 64, 68-69, 96
experiential-expressivism, 89-90, 97
explanation, 9, 52, 55, 60-67, 98
extrabiblical, extratextual, 30, 60-67, 87, 94-96, 98
faith, 27, 102, 112
fête du sens, 50, 67, 82, 119
fideism, 5
figure, figuration. *See* trope, tropology
form/content, 17, 36, 55-60
Ford, David, 2, 52, 95
foundationalism, xiv, 88, 94, 96-103, 110, 112, 117, 122
Frei, Hans, xiv, 1-2, 41-45, 63, 87, 90-110, 112
Frye, Northrop, 21-23

Gadamer, Hans-Georg, 5, 29, 43, 56
Geertz, Clifford, 26, 89
gender-bias, 113, 118
Genesis creation accounts, 10-11, 40, 73-78, 99
genre analysis, 33, 41, 56
God. *See* Barth and God; naming God; Ricoeur and God
Gospel, the, 29, 54, 101
gospels, 42, 50, 82-85
grace, 16, 116
grammar, 89-96, 105
Gustafson, James, 77-78

Heidegger, Martin, 61, 72, 96
Heilsgeschichte, 42, 74
hermeneutics, 1-2, 5, 96
general and special, 64-67, 70-71, 79, 122
threefold method, xiv, 52-72, 81-82
See also Barth and hermeneutics; Ricoeur and hermeneutics
Hirsch, E. D., Jr., 34
historical criticism, viii, xii, xiii, 51, 71, 92, 113. *See also* Barth and historical criticism; Ricoeur and historical criticism
historicism, 8, 10, 13, 21, 66-67, 121, 123
history, 24, 29, 37, 66-69, 91-92, 121-22
historylike, 10, 42, 91
Holmer, Paul, xiv, 87, 92-96, 103-105
Holy Spirit, 2, 3, 7-8, 24-25, 111
hope, 112

intentional fallacy. *See* authorial intention
intertextual, 13, 41, 50, 66-67, 71, 73, 112, 118
intratextual, intrabiblical, 30, 63, 82, 87-96, 103, 104, 112, 114
Iser, Wolfgang, 43

Jauss, Hans-Robert, 43
Jesus Christ. *See* Barth and Jesus Christ; Ricoeur and Jesus Christ
Judas, xiii, 20-21, 45
Jüngel, Eberhard, 3, 12, 26, 102

Kelsey, David, 87-88
Kermode, Frank, 44-45, 46-48
kerygma, 26, 36, 45, 47, 53-55, 59
Klemm, David, 29, 55

lament, 82-85
language-game. *See* Wittgenstein, Ludwig
Lessing, Gotthold Ephraim, 68-69
Leviticus, Book of, xiii, 71
liberalism, xii, 88, 90, 96-97, 123
Lindbeck, George, xiv, 63, 87-110, 112, 117, 124
literary criticism, 2, 6, 22, 24, 44-50, 66-67, 74-78, 121-22

Mabee, Charles, 124
manifestation, 37-40
Mark, Gospel of, xiv, 37, 40-50, 71, 118
metacriticism, xiii, 12-13, 20
mimesis, 56, 69
modernism, xii, 59, 71, 72, 117
Moltmann, Jürgen, 96
mystery, 39-40, 41, 48, 84, 113
myth, 10, 54-55, 58

naiveté, viii, 12-13, 26, 57, 67, 123
second (critical), viii, xiii-xv, 51, 70-72, 111-25
naming God, xiii, 29-30, 64, 81
narrative, 40-50, 89-92, 98, 100
narrative theology. *See* theology and narrative
narratology. *See* narrative
nature. *See* ecology
neoorthodoxy, 42, 113, 118, 120
neo-Protestantism, xii, 62
neo-Thomism, xii, 113, 120
New Criticism, 13, 21, 23, 34, 112